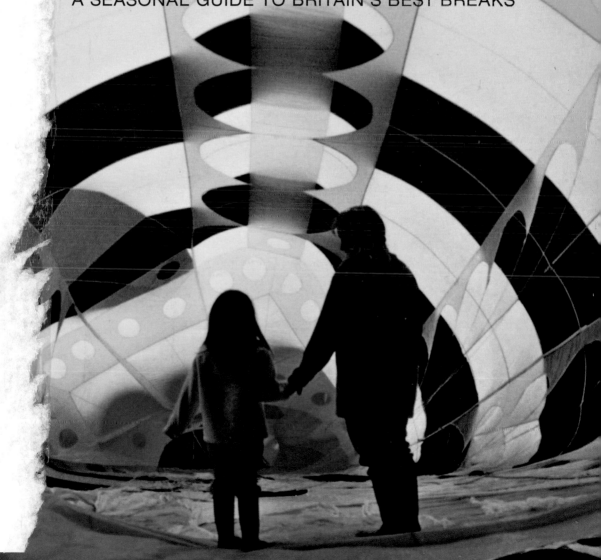

52 Great British
WEEKENDS

A SEASONAL GUIDE TO BRITAIN'S BEST BREAKS

52 Great British
WEEKENDS

A SEASONAL GUIDE TO BRITAIN'S BEST BREAKS

Annabelle Thorpe

NEW HOLLAND

For my Mum, who always loved autumn best.

Published in 2012
by New Holland Publishers (UK) Ltd
London • Cape Town • Sydney • Auckland

www.newhollandpublishers.com

Garfield House, 86–88 Edgware Road,
London W2 2EA, United Kingdom

80 McKenzie Street, Cape Town 8001, South Africa

Unit 1, 66 Gibbes Street, Chatswood, NSW 2067,
Australia

218 Lake Road, Northcote, Auckland, New Zealand

ISBN 978 1 84773 948 3

Publisher: Guy Hobbs
Project editor: Sally MacEachern
Proofreader: Elspeth Anderson
Designer: Isobel Gillan
Picture research: Susannah Jayes
Cartography: Stephen Dew
Production: Marion Storz

Reproduction by Modern Age Repro House Ltd,
Hong Kong
Printed and bound by Toppan Leefung Printing Ltd,
China

Although the publishers have made every effort to
ensure that information contained in this book was
researched and correct at the time of going to press,
they accept no responsibility for any inaccuracies,
loss, injury or inconvenience sustained by any
person using this book as reference.

spring

summer

autumn

winter

Introduction

Live in each season as it passes; breathe the air, drink the drink, taste the fruit and resign yourself to the influences of each.

HENRY DAVID THOREAU

To live in each season as it passes; is there any other way on our windswept, sun-kissed, chilly, sultry island? The weather holds an unending fascination for us Brits, but no wonder: winter brings blizzards and bright blue skies, while spring offers torrential showers and glorious sunny days that make us rush to dust off the barbecue and head to the beaches in our millions. As for summer, who can predict? The reservoirs may dry up or overflow, the tennis courts at Wimbledon may be hot with sunshine or hidden from rain. And then autumn, rich in golden hues and soft sunlight, the last days of warmth giving way to crisp, cold air thick with early morning mist in the fields and the bittersweet smell of bonfires.

And for each season there are traditions to observe and natural wonders to marvel at: winter skies thick with thousands of migrating birds, spring streets peppered with vivid pink cherry blossom, tiptoeing into the sea in summer, walking beneath flame-coloured trees in the autumn months. Our food, culture, history and landscapes are indelibly entwined with the changing seasons which shape our island home, reinventing it anew through every stage of the year.

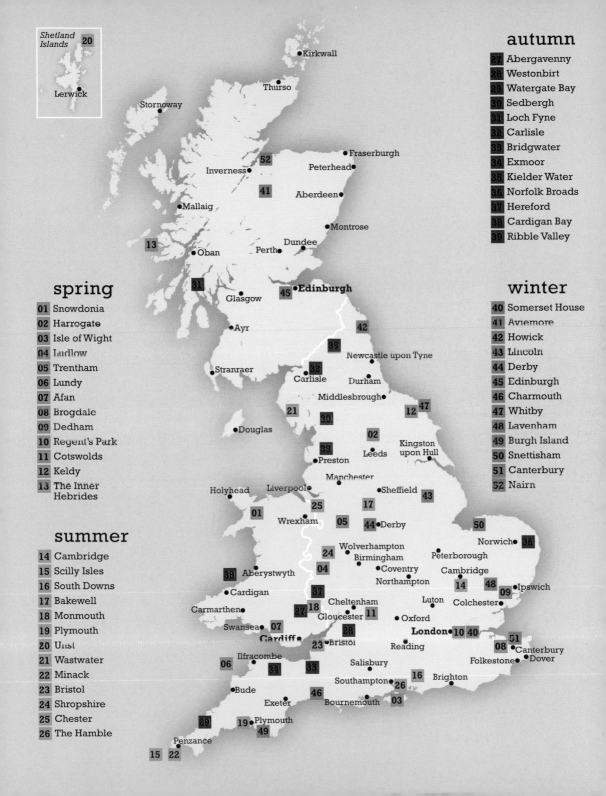

Shetland Islands [20]

Lerwick

autumn

27	Abergavenny
28	Westonbirt
29	Watergate Bay
30	Sedbergh
31	Loch Fyne
32	Carlisle
33	Bridgwater
34	Exmoor
35	Kielder Water
36	Norfolk Broads
37	Hereford
38	Cardigan Bay
39	Ribble Valley

spring

01	Snowdonia
02	Harrogate
03	Isle of Wight
04	Ludlow
05	Trentham
06	Lundy
07	Afan
08	Brogdale
09	Dedham
10	Regent's Park
11	Cotswolds
12	Keldy
13	The Inner Hebrides

summer

14	Cambridge
15	Scilly Isles
16	South Downs
17	Bakewell
18	Monmouth
19	Plymouth
20	Unst
21	Wastwater
22	Minack
23	Bristol
24	Shropshire
25	Chester
26	The Hamble

winter

40	Somerset House
41	Aviemore
42	Howick
43	Lincoln
44	Derby
45	Edinburgh
46	Charmouth
47	Whitby
48	Lavenham
49	Burgh Island
50	Snettisham
51	Canterbury
52	Nairn

Kirkwall
Thurso
Stornoway
Fraserburgh
Inverness · [52] · Peterhead
[41] · Aberdeen
Mallaig · Montrose
Oban · Dundee
[13] · Perth
Glasgow · [45] · **Edinburgh**
[31]
Ayr · [42]
Stranraer · [35] · Newcastle upon Tyne
[32] · Durham
Carlisle · Middlesbrough · [47]
[21] · [30] · [12]
Douglas · [02]
[39] · Leeds · Kingston upon Hull
Preston · Manchester
Holyhead · Liverpool · Sheffield · [43]
[01] · [25] · [17]
Wrexham · [05] · [44] · Derby
[24] · Wolverhampton · [50]
[38] Aberystwyth · Birmingham · Norwich · [36]
[04] · Coventry · Peterborough
Cardigan · Northampton · Cambridge
Carmarthen · [37] · Cheltenham · [14] · [48]
Swansea · [27] [18] · Luton · Colchester · [09] · Ipswich
[07] · Gloucester · [11] · Oxford
Cardiff · [28] · London · [10] [40]
[23] · Bristol · [08] · [51]
[06] · Reading · Canterbury
Ilfracombe · Salisbury · Folkestone · Dover
[34] · [33] · [16]
Bude · Southampton · [26] · Brighton
[46] · Bournemouth · [03]
[29] · [19] Plymouth · Exeter
Penzance · [49]
[15] [22]

spring

The most joyous of the seasons, spring begins with the violet crocuses pushing up through the frosty soil, quickly followed by buttery daffodils, scarlet tulips and lush banks of bluebells. As the days lengthen, even the most urban streets are blessed with beauty, as almond and cherry trees blossom pink and white and bare branches burst into leaf. Now is the time to dig out the walking boots and head for the hills, when the landscapes are in their first flush of beauty and optimism is in the air.

01 Stride Up Snowdon
SNOWDONIA, WALES

Lace up your boots for a memorable hike up Wales's most spectacular mountain (or, if you're feeling lazy, let the train take the strain).

It's only when you venture deep into Wales that you get the sense of its deep-rooted identity and sense of otherness. The Snowdonia National Park is an area steeped in Welsh traditions and heritage, and over half the population who live within the 207 sq. km (800 sq. miles) of the park speak Welsh. It is one of the most spectacular corners of our country, home to the highest mountain and largest lake in Wales, with vast wooded hills rolling out towards snow-capped peaks, with villages and sleepy hamlets dotted among the valleys and slopes.

Snowdonia is a place to discover Wales's long history, with Stone Age burial chambers, Roman forts, churches, castles and slate quarries dotted through the wide-screen landscapes. A walk in Snowdonia can take in millions of years of history, whether on a short stroll across the hills or a more hard-core trek up one of the six paths that lead to the summit of Mount Snowdon itself.

Climbing Mount Snowdon is not something that should be taken on lightly. The six paths differ in length and difficulty: Llanberis is the longest and, in warmer weather, the easiest, while the Pyg path is one of the steepest and most difficult, particularly in the winter months. Although the longest trail is only 8km (5 miles), it's important to remember that the effort comes in the gradient, rather than the length of the walk. It's imperative to climb in proper walking shoes and, even if the spring sunshine is warm, to carry a warm sweater, as it can be nine degrees cooler at the summit, which reaches 1,085m (3,560ft).

The good news, however, is that you can reach the top without having to even lace up your walking boots. The Snowdonia Mountain Railway (snowdonrailway.co.uk) has been carrying visitors up the mountain

OPPOSITE: Hikers tackling Mount Snowdon's steep paths are rewarded by some of the best views in Britain.

since 1896, and is the only public rack-and-pinion railway in the UK. An added bonus is the spectacular visitor centre, which opened in 2009, complete with historical displays, local information and a cafe that makes the most of the 'wall of glass' that affords the most astonishing views across the peaks.

For younger families there are plenty of other options to explore in the national park. The Greenwood Forest Park (greenwoodforestpark.co.uk) combines roller-coaster rides with archery, treetops and tunnel play areas and a Forest Theatre that hosts daily performances in the school summer holidays. Older kids will be fascinated by the Centre of Alternative Technology (cat.org.uk), one of the world's most renowned eco-centres, with slug and bug hunts for young children, an interactive theatre and interactive displays and exhibits on sustainable living.

But for many visitors to Snowdonia, it is the spectacular natural landscapes that are the major draw. Whether pottering around the picturesque streets of Betws y Coed, the air thick with the impenetrable Welsh language, exploring one of the 13th-century castles that dot the hills or enduring the long pull up to the top of Mount Snowdon itself, there is nowhere better to experience the real Wales – a different country without leaving home.

LEFT: *The picturesque, stone-built village of Beddgelert, just south of Snowdon, is in the midst of magnificent hiking country. The less energetic visitor can hop on a steam train, as Beddgelert is one of the stops on the spectacular Welsh Highland Railway.*
RIGHT: *Cwm Pennant is often called 'the most beautiful valley in Wales'. It is bordered on three sides by mountains and is the source of the Dwyfor River, which meanders past the occasional farm house and an ancient church. Busy with slate workings in the 19th century, today the valley slopes are dotted with cattle and sheep. Spring, when bluebells cover the valley sides, is the best time to visit.*

INFORMATION

STAY Camp in style in one of the canvas yurts at **Graig Wen** (01341 250482; graigwen.co.uk), which come with wood-burning stove, futon beds, rugs and floor cushions – with Welsh breakfast hampers available. In the heart of Snowdonia, **St Curig's Church** (01690 720469; stcurigschurch.com) is a converted 19th-century chapel with spectacular rooms, and a dining area in what was once the apse. Lux it up at **Tyn Rhos Country House** (01248 670489; tynrhos.co.uk) in nearby Llanddeiniolen, which offers cosy but elegant rooms.

EAT Reward yourself after a Snowdon hike with lunch at **Caban** (01286 685500; caban-cyf.org/EN), a fabulous cafe near the foot of the mountain that grows most of the ingredients used. Much loved by locals and climbers, **Pete's Eats** (01286 870117; petes-eats.co.uk) is famous for its huge portions of healthy food (including lots of veggie options) at affordable prices. In the heart of the national park, **Peak** (01286 872777; peakrestaurant.co.uk) is one of the most popular in the area, specializing in traditional dishes with a modern twist.

MORE INFO eryri.npa.gov.uk

GETTING THERE Take the A458 west from Welshpool, or the A5 west from Oswestry.

OTHER GREAT CLIMBS
• Ben Nevis, Scotland (fortwilliam.co.uk)
• Scafell Pike, Cumbria (golakes.co.uk)
• The Munros, Scotland (munromagic.com)

02 Take Tea at Bettys
HARROGATE, ENGLAND

Choose from over 300 mouthwatering varieties of cake and 50 types of tea at this legendary Yorkshire tea shop in the heart of the Dales.

Forget Starbucks, Costa and all those other chain coffee shops which serve buckets of lukewarm lattes and silly, skinny, double-decaf cappuccinos. At heart we remain a nation of tea drinkers – a reassuring cuppa as much a part of our national psyche as losing at football and barbecuing in the rain. So what better way to celebrate St George's Day (23 April) than with a slap-up afternoon tea at Bettys in Harrogate, one of the oldest and most celebrated tea shops in the country.

Bettys (bettys.co.uk) may now have six branches in Yorkshire, but the first to open, in 1919, was the creation of a Swiss traveller, Frederick Belmont. In those days Harrogate was a fashionable spa town, and Frederick decided to open a cafe using the knowledge he had gained as an apprentice to bakers and confectioners in Europe. Combining Swiss culinary flair and a warm Yorkshire welcome proved a winner, and the cafe was an instant success. He went on to open other branches of Bettys, including a flagship tea room in York. Years later, the basement Bettys Bar became a huge favourite with Canadian and US soldiers stationed nearby during the war.

Twenty-first-century Bettys retains much of its original charm, and the accent is still on handmade pastries and cakes (over 300 to choose from), washed down with one of over 50 teas and coffees. Located on Parliament Street, it's the perfect stop-off after a morning exploring the elegant town of Harrogate, famed for its elegant, wide streets and Georgian terraces. A stroll down the hill from Bettys lies the picturesque Montpellier Quarter, home to antique shops, art galleries and the Royal Pump Room Museum (harrogate.gov.uk), which gives an insight into the town's spa heritage.

TOP LEFT: Silver cake stands piled high with goodies. TOP RIGHT: Bettys Café Tearooms' distinctive wrought-iron canopy with its colourful hanging baskets. BOTTOM: Thousands of crocuses carpet the Stray in spring.

The beauty of a spring break in Harrogate is that you can combine indulgent afternoon teas and shopping sprees with hearty walks in the stunning surrounding countryside. Harrogate is close to both the Yorkshire Dales National Park (yorkshiredales.org.uk) and the Nidderdale AONB (nidderdaleaonb.org.uk). Both areas are criss-crossed with walking and cycling routes, offering everything from taxing hikes to gentle strolls. For something a little different you can join a llama trek across Nidderdale (nidderdalellamas.org) or follow some of the white-knuckle mountain bike trails.

On a warm spring day, one of the most beautiful places to visit near Harrogate is Ripley Castle (ripleycastle.co.uk), owned by the same family for over 700 years. Ripley has played host to an array of historical figures from James I to Oliver Cromwell, and the seven rooms that are open to the public offer a fascinating insight into past eras. In the spring months, the gardens are ablaze with colour: thousands of daffodil, narcissi and tulips, along with carpets of bluebells and flaming rhododendrons.

Harrogate offers an unbeatable mix of urban style and rural pleasures – the perfect weekend combination.

INFORMATION

STAY A B&B with the feel of a stylish boutique hotel, the **Bijou** (01423 567974; thebijou.co.uk) has 10 individually designed en suite rooms with lots of luxury touches. For an indulgent getaway, **Hotel du Vin** (0845 365 4438; hotelduvin.com) has 48 rooms in a row of Georgian houses overlooking the Stray, an 80-ha (200-acre) common. Campers and caravanners should head to **High Moor Farm Park** (01423 563637; highmoorfarmpark.co.uk), just 6km (4 miles) from Harrogate, surrounded by gorgeous Dales countryside.

EAT If you've room after all the tea and cake at Bettys, book a table at the **Harrogate Brasserie** (01423 505041; harrogatebrasserie. co.uk), which has live jazz at the weekend and a seasonal menu of hearty dishes. If you're out exploring the countryside, pop into the **Malt Shovel** (01423 862929; themaltshovelbrearton. co.uk) – renowned for its carefully prepared dishes made with local produce – for an indulgent lunch. For an elegant supper, try **Sasso** (01423 508838; sasso restaurant.co.uk), where chef and co-owner Stefano Lancellotti brings a little piece of Italy to the streets of Harrogate.

GETTING THERE Leave the A1 (M) at Junction 46 and follow the A658 to a junction with the A59. Follow the A59 to Harrogate.

MORE INFO
yorkshire.com/do/places/harrogate

OTHER TEA SHOPS
• Sally Lunns, Bath, Wiltshire (sallylunns.co.uk)
• St James's Room, Fortnum & Mason, London (fortnumandmason.com)
• Orchard Tea Garden, Cambridge (orchard-grantchester.com)

03 Walk the Wight
ISLE OF WIGHT, ENGLAND

Head to Hampshire to join the biggest walking festival in the country, with more than 800 km (500 miles) of footpaths to explore.

For many people who grew up in the south of England, the Isle of Wight is a nostalgic place, full of childhood memories of bucket-and-spade holidays, ice cream and candyfloss, strolls on piers and rainy nights under canvas. This diamond-shaped piece of land, just 5km (3 miles) from the English coast, has been drawing visitors since Queen Victoria's time, when she had the elegant Osborne House built so that she and Prince Albert and their seven children could take family holidays on the island.

Like all islands, the Wight has a very particular feeling. In some ways visiting the island is a trip back into the past; the pace of life is slower, pleasures simpler, even the bigger towns such as Ryde and Newport have a deliciously old-fashioned feel. But as a holiday destination, the IOW has reinvented itself in recent years as more

RIGHT: The Needles is just one of the many visual treats awaiting hikers on the Isle of Wight.

than just family-friendly; boutique hotels and gastropubs have sprung up across the island, linked by a network of footpaths.

Walking is big business for islanders. There are more miles of footpaths than roads and every May the island is flooded by hearty types clutching maps and fleeces who come for the annual walking festival (isleofwightwalkingfestival.co.uk). It's a great time to visit, with dozens of organized walks and themed events.

The longest trail around the island is the Isle of Wight Coastal Path, which stretches for 108km (67 miles) of well-maintained paths. The path can be broken down in sections that are easily do-able in a day; the 13km (8-mile) route from Niton to Sandown takes in some lovely stretches of beach

ABOVE: The historic New Inn at Shalfleet dates from 1743. OPPOSITE: Hikers stride out along the Tennyson Trail.

around Ventnor and Shanklin, while a route of the same length from Ryde to Cowes takes in Osborne House, the ruins of 12th-century Quarr Abbey and the villages of Wootton and Fishbourne.

There are also eight inland trails that take in some of the most rural and beautiful areas of the island: the Shepherds Trail starts at the famous Carisbrooke Castle and rises up over the hills to give beautiful views, while the Tennyson Trail is one of the most challenging and spectacular, stretching 22.5km (14 miles) from Carisbrooke, up and over the downs to the Needles, and finishing at Alum Bay.

INFORMATION

STAY Those in search of a decadent weekend should book the **Hambrough** (01983 856333; thehambrough.com) in Ventnor; just seven slick bedrooms and a renowned restaurant overlooking the sea. The island is dotted with campsites; one of the best is **Southlands** (01983 865385), a beautifully manicured site with excellent facilities. For a foodie break, stay at the **Seaview** (01983 612711; seaviewhotel.co.uk), which serves dishes made with produce from the hotel's own farm. There's also a beauty and treatment room to soothe tired limbs after a day's walking.

EAT Warm up post-walk with a bowl of seafood chowder at the perfectly located **Spyglass Inn** (01983 855338; thespyglass.com) at the tip of Ventnor's esplanade, right on the sea. The **New Inn** at Shalfleet (01983 531314; the new-inn.co.uk) is an ideal mix of walker's country inn and gastropub, serving up fab Sunday lunches. Indulge in a classic cream tea at **Warren Farm Tea Rooms** (farmhousecreamteas.co.uk), with great views out over Alum Bay.

GETTING THERE Wightlink (0871 376 1000; wightlink.co.uk) runs ferries to the island from Portsmouth and Lymington. Red Funnel (redfunnel.co.uk) runs ferries from Southampton.

MORE INFO islandbreaks.co.uk

OTHER GREAT SPRING WALKING FESTIVALS
• The North Devon and Exmoor Walking Festival (exmoorwalkingfestival.co.uk)
• The Lincolnshire Wolds Walking Festival (woldswalkingfestival.co.uk)
• Walk Scilly (simplyscilly.co.uk)

Alongside walking there is plenty to see and do on the island. Kids will love the old-fashioned theme park at Blackgang Chine (blackgangchine.com) and Dinosaur Isle (dinosaurisle.com) near Sandown. For more adult pleasures, Rosemary Vineyard (rosemaryvineyard.co.uk) offers tours and tastings, while foodies can follow the Wight Taste Trail that takes in local farm shops, organic producers and pubs.

But one of the greatest pleasures is discovering the island's sleepy villages – particularly in the spring months before the crowds arrive. Browse the art galleries in Yarmouth, potter around the gift shops in Godshill or stroll the picturesque streets of Shanklin Old Village, and let the old-fashioned charms of island life slowly work their magic.

04 Dine Out in Style
LUDLOW, ENGLAND

From Michelin-starred eateries to gastropubs and farm shops, this picturesque Shropshire town is the perfect choice for a foodie weekend.

For a small, sleepy town on the England-Wales border, Ludlow's rise to fame as Britain's rural gastro-capital is something of an achievement. Surrounded by the lush agricultural countryside of the Marches, the town is a central point for local produce and a wide variety of traditional and exotic ingredients are on offer at the delis, restaurants and speciality producers that dot the town. Home to the country's first-ever food festival, which takes place in the autumn, the town is an all-round foodie treat, and in spring fresh produce floods into the shops.

The poet John Betjeman once described Ludlow as the 'loveliest town in England' and with over 500 listed buildings – some half-timbered, some Georgian – it remains a charming place to visit, steeped in history. The medieval streets are overlooked by Ludlow Castle (ludlowcastle.com), which dates back to the 11th century and is a fascinating place to visit, with grounds and rooms that give a feel of how life would have been some 500 years ago.

There are currently seven restaurants in and around the town that have entries in the Michelin guide, but there are also plenty of more informal, less pricey establishments. Ludlow is also a great place for a self-catering break, with wonderful delis and speciality food shops throughout the town: pop into the Deli on the Square (4 Church Street), D Wall & Sons for fabulous sausages (14 High Street) and the Little Big Cheese Shop (Corve Street).

There is also a thrice-weekly market (Mondays, Fridays and Saturdays) that combines local produce – cheese, breads, meats – with books and local crafts. The local farmers' market, held on the second

TOP LEFT: The market dates back 900 years. TOP RIGHT: Deli on the Square offers over 140 varieties of cheese. BOTTOM: Ludlow Castle is at the heart of the town.

INFORMATION

STAY The beauty of Ludlow is that some of its best eating establishments also offer rooms. **De Greys** (01584 872764; degreys.co.uk) in an Elizabethan town house is a classic tea room, but also has nine luxury bedrooms upstairs. **Mr Underhills** (01584 874431; mr-underhills.co.uk) is a Michelin-starred restaurant idyllically situated on the banks of the river Teme, offering sleek, indulgent bedrooms and a self-catering cottage. Self-catering is a great option in Ludlow; **Corve Street Cottage** is a cosy 17th-century cottage in the centre of the town, just one of several available through Cottages4you (cottages4you.co.uk)

EAT Slip into a bygone age with afternoon tea at **Rocke Cottage Tea Room** (rockecottagetearoom. co.uk), where the home-made cakes and over 20 varieties of tea are served against a soundtrack of gentle music from the 1920s and 1930s. For a really special meal, Michelin-starred **La Becasse** (01584 872325; labecasse.co.uk) serves spectacular food under the careful hand of head chef Will Holland, but keeps a pleasingly relaxed feel for such an upscale restaurant. For a classic pub lunch, the **Unicorn** (01584 873555; unicorn-ludlow.co.uk) offers hefty sandwiches and full meals.

GETTING THERE Leave the M5 at Junction 7, follow the A440 and then the A44 through Worcester. At Leominster take to A49 to Ludlow.

MORE INFO ludlow.org.uk

OTHER RURAL MICHELIN EATERIES
• The Hand & Flowers, Marlow, Bucks (thehandandflowers.co.uk)
• The Neptune Inn, Hunstanton, Norfolk (theneptune.co.uk)
• The Star Inn, Harome, Yorkshire (thestaratharome.co.uk)

and fourth Thursdays of every month, offers great foodie shopping potential, with 20 to 30 stalls selling produce from within a 32-km (20-mile) radius of Ludlow.

If you need to walk off all the good food, there are some lovely walks that start from the heart of Ludlow. The Mortimer Trail is a 48-km (30-mile) route which begins in Ludlow and runs along a series of ridges to the border town of Kington, while the Shropshire Way (shropshirewalking.co.uk/shropshire-way/) passes through the town, with spectacular walks either north to Bromfield or east to Titterstone Clee Hill. For a short stroll, Whitcliff Common is a mixture of woods and grassland that lies above the river Teme, and gives fantastic views of the old town centre.

Further afield the Shropshire Hills are an AONB (shropshirehills.info), home to picturesque historic villages such as Clun and the atmospheric Long Mynd, a spectacular 16km- (10 mile-) long mountain that offers panoramic views and is a great place to walk. Owned by the National Trust, for information on how to get out and explore the Long Mynd, head to Carding Mill Valley, where there is an excellent visitor centre. Whether you choose to explore the tranquil Shropshire countryside on foot or horseback, or by bike or car, just make sure you take a picnic with you.

05 Monkey Around
TRENTHAM, ENGLAND

Explore the unique Monkey World at Staffordshire's beautiful Trentham Estate, a tribe of 140 Barbary Macaques rule the roost.

It's coming to something when you can't find space on a picnic bench because a family of monkeys have got there first. But in the Trentham Monkey Forest, a 24-ha (60-acre) stretch of Staffordshire woodland, this is exactly how things are supposed to be.

In the Forest, the tribe of Barbary macaques live freely, with as little intervention as possible by humans. Visitors can watch the

BELOW: Where else could you eyeball a monkey at such close quarters?

ABOVE: *In the spring months, Trentham Gardens bursts into life.*

monkeys feeding, take photographs or sit beside them (if you can find room) but the natural habitats of the monkeys must not be disturbed.

A winding 1.2km (¾ mile) path takes visitors through the woodlands, where monkeys roam freely. There are plenty of guides on hand to answer questions, give more information about the monkeys and explain their different behaviours. Late spring is an ideal time to visit, as this tends to be when the baby macaques are born: tiny inquisitive creatures, who charm both adults and children. Alongside the forest

there are two adventure playgrounds for kids, and a pretty picnic area (food must not be taken into the monkeys' home).

The Monkey Forest is just one of several attractions at the massive Trentham Estate. The historic Italian garden is one of the most impressive stately gardens in Britain; originally designed by Capability Brown for the Duke of Sutherland in the mid-18th century, it surrounds a mile-long lake. The gardens have been carefully restored in recent years, and alongside the formal planting, there are prairies to walk through, the 'Hide and Speak' maze to get lost in, and Britain's first barefoot walk. If it's a warm day, a cruise on the lake is an ideal option, while younger kids will love the chance to ride on the 'Trentham Fern' – the estate's own miniature railway.

Staffordshire is one of the best areas of Britain for a family break; home to the country's biggest theme park, Alton Towers (altontowers.com), as well as the smaller Drayton Manor (draytonmanor.co.uk). Less overwhelming and frenetic than its glitzier sister, Drayton Manor is a great bet for younger families, with plenty of gentle rides and a small zoo, as well as terrifying roller coasters and vertical-drop rides. For a wet and wild time, Waterworld (waterworld.co.uk) is the UK's largest indoor aqua theme park, with over 30 rides and an aqua disco.

A short drive from Trentham, the small city of Stoke-on-Trent is well worth a visit (visitstoke.co.uk). Famous for its potteries,

Stoke is known as the world capital of ceramics, and is home to famous names such as Wedgwood, Emma Bridgewater, Portmeirion and Dalby. The £10m Wedgwood Museum (wedgwoodmuseum. org.uk) gives a fascinating insight into the history of pottery in the region, which started with Josiah Wedgwood who founded the company in 1759. There are also over 25 factory shops to visit, with famous brands offering seconds at vastly reduced prices – and many also offer tours, allowing visitors to see the skill that goes into producing the china for which Stoke is rightly famed.

RIGHT: Drop, twist and turn on Drayton Park's thrilling G-Force roller coaster.

INFORMATION

STAY Stay right by Trentham Estate in budget choice **Premier Inn** (0871 527 9050; premierinn.com), great for a family break. Discover Staffordshire's tranquil countryside with a stay at **Highfields Farm** (01889 505000; highfields-bb.co.uk), which has five cosy rooms in converted barns and offers a fantastic farm-fresh breakfast. The **Graythwaite** (01782 612875; thegraythwaite.co.uk) is a stylish B&B in Newcastle-under-Lyme, with chic modern rooms and an award-winning breakfast.

EAT After an energetic day at Trentham, refuel with some good, old-fashioned pub grub at the **Three Crowns** (01785 819516; vintageinn.co.uk) in the nearby village of Stone. Flagged floors, old beams and exposed brickwork give the pub a rustic, welcoming feel. The Trentham Estate has a clutch of eating options: treat the kids to home-made ice creams and sundaes at **Cadwaladers Ice Cream** (01782 654177). For a lively evening out, **Granville's Brasserie** (01785 816658; granvilles.st) offers live music alongside an inventive menu and an extensive wine list.

MORE INFO trentham.co.uk

GETTING THERE Leave the M6 at Junction 15 and follow the A500 and then the A34 to Trentham.

OTHER GREAT ANIMAL PARKS
• Longleat Safari Park, Wiltshire (longleat.co.uk)
• Woburn Safari Park, Bucks (woburn.co.uk/safari)
• Galloway Wildlife Conservation Park, Dumfries and Galloway (gallowaywildlife.co.uk)

06 Escape to an Island
LUNDY, ENGLAND

Forget the mobile and the laptop and leave the Devonshire coast behind to hole up for a tranquil weekend on wild and rural Lundy Island.

Eating out on Lundy Island is an uncomplicated business: the Marisco Tavern or the Marisco Tavern? There is just one pub on the island, just as there is one shop, one church, one castle, and one working farm. There is also very little mobile coverage, limited electricity (so no television) and just 27 permanent residents. If you want a break that offers an escape from the pressures of modern-day life, there's no better place than Lundy.

Situated 18km (11 miles) off the Devon coast, the island is accessible by boat from March through October (the crossing is by helicopter in winter). It's worth noting however, that the seas can be ferociously choppy, so arriving by air can be a preferable option, even in the summer months. Once there, however, all is peace and calm. Just 5km (3 miles) long and 0.8km (½ mile) wide, Lundy has a very particular atmosphere – a tiny drop of Britain where time really has stood still.

The island has a chequered history. Once used as a granite quarry, it was granted to the Knights Templar by Henry II in 1160, but became a favoured spot for pirates, who took advantage of the fact that ships were forced to navigate close to Lundy because of the dangerous shingle banks in the fast-flowing river Severn. In the 18th and early 19th century it became increasingly lawless and exchanged hands several times before finally being given to the National Trust, who leased it to the Landmark Trust.

Self-catering is the only option on the island, and the Landmark Trust owns 23 properties – ranging from the very basic, with no electricity, to more comfortable. Days on Lundy are spent walking and wildlife-spotting – the island is a Site of Special Interest and the waters around it are

OPPOSITE: The waters below Gannet's Rock Pinnacle offer superb diving.

INFORMATION

STAY Lundy is unique in that the 23 places to stay on the island are all owned by the Landmark Trust (01628 825925; landmarktrust. org.uk). **Government House**, which sleeps five, and was built to house the person responsible for running Lundy, is now the Landmark's finest house on the island. Couples can stay in the **Old School**, a vividly painted building known locally as the 'blue bung', which offers cosy, charming accommodation. For a bit of drama that the kids will love, stay at **Castle Keep South**, a stone-built cottage in the castle which sleeps four.

EAT There is only one place to eat on the island: the **Marisco Tavern,** which opens up for breakfast every day and keeps going through coffees and cakes, lunches, dinners and plenty of Lundy Light ale in between (sadly now brewed on the mainland). There is also the local village shop, which sells most of the necessary provisions for satisfactory self-catering, including the world-famous Lundy Lamb.

MORE INFO lundyisland.co.uk

GETTING THERE By helicopter from Hartland Point from November to March, and from Bideford or Ilfracombe on the MS *Oldenburg* in the summer months. Book both on 01271 863636.

OTHER ISLAND ESCAPES
• Lindisfarne, Northumberland (lindisfarne.org.uk)
• The Isles of Scilly, Cornwall (simplyscilly.co.uk)
• Mersea Island, Essex (mersea-island.com)

INSET OPPOSITE: Lundy is an old Norse word meaning 'puffin.' OPPOSITE: It's a steep walk up from the jetty. ABOVE: Guillemots cluster on the rocky outcrops.

England's only statutory marine reserve. Basking sharks, seals and dolphins are often seen in the sea, while guillemots, razorbills and peregrine falcons wheel around in the skies above. Late spring is famous for providing sanctuary to thousands of nesting birds, particularly puffins, and from Easter onwards there is a programme of walks, talks and snorkelling safaris led by the island's warden.

One of the greatest joys of Lundy is simply being out and about in the warm spring sunshine, strolling along the dramatic coastline or settling down with a picnic somewhere like Brazen Ward, on the east coast, where seals can often be seen playing in the surrounding waters. On a blustery day there is no more spectacular spot than the very north-eastern tip of the island where the Atlantic meets the Bristol Channel – and on a quiet day you may well have the area to yourself.

Twitchers – and puffin-spotters in particular – should settle in for the morning at Jenny's Cove, on the western shore, where the birds are often seen. But to rush round the island ticking off sightings is to miss the point of this unique place; the delight of Lundy is its joyous insistence on visitors doing not very much of anything at all.

07 Get on Your Bike
AFAN, WALES

Pack helmet and knee pads for a white-knuckle ride on some of the fierce bike trails in this tranquil corner of the Welsh valleys. Or, take it easy with a gentle pedal along a former railway line.

On a warm spring day, with trees bursting into leaf and clusters of bluebells jigging in the breeze, there are few places more beautiful than the Welsh valleys. Lush with meadows and ancient woodland, dotted with sleepy mining villages, nature has gradually reclaimed these hills and valleys from the industries that once defined them, and where once the air was thick with grime and soot from the mines, it is now crisp and clear.

Communities in the Welsh valleys are increasingly welcoming to visitors, with excellent accommodation springing up in the towns and villages, and new walking, cycling and horse-riding trails beginning to cross the natural landscapes. For those who love to explore on two wheels, Wales is the perfect choice – and those in search of both breathtaking scenery, and an equally breathtaking ride, should head to the Afan Forest Park in the Welsh valleys, one of the most beautiful stretches of wild countryside in the country.

Afan has trails for all levels of cyclist, whether you're after high-octane mountain biking or gentle family routes. There are five world-class trails, 'Penhydd', 'Y Wal', 'Skyline', 'White's Level' and 'W2', which together boast over 100km (60 miles) of single-track trails. Twisting through trees, sharp climbs into exposed hillsides and steep descents into wooded valleys, these routes will satisfy the most hardcore of bikers, and are the reason Afan has been voted one of the 10 places in the world to 'ride before you die'.

For those after something gentler, the 'Y Rheilfford' trail runs along a former railway line. The 36-km (22-mile) route is reassuringly flat, making it ideal for families, and there are plenty of picnic spots along the way. In the heart of the park lies the Glyncorrwg Mountain Bike Centre, where

OPPOSITE: Just choose your trail grade and distance and you're off – Afan Forest Park has bike trails for all ages and all stages of fitness.

you can hire bikes, stop for lunch or even pitch your tent and extend your time in the forest. There are also three ponds for fishing and water activities.

Outside the park, there's plenty to explore in the surrounding area. If you've got the kids in tow, one of the best attractions in the area is Margam Country Park (npt.gov.uk), just outside Port Talbot. The adventure playground, narrow-gauge railway and farm trail should keep the young ones happy, while there's 324ha (800 acres) of gardens surrounding the castle and ornamental gardens – plenty of room for yomping around and recovering with a picnic.

Alternatively, head to the beach and explore the Merthyr Mawr Sand Dunes;

ABOVE: Aberavon Beach, near Port Talbot, is popular with surfers and kitesurfers.
OPPOSITE: Sgwd yr Pannwr waterfalls on the river Mellte.

home of the largest sand dunes in Europe, Merthyr was the location for the desert scenes in *Lawrence of Arabia*. There are literally miles of dunes to explore, and children will love hopping across the stepping stones to Ogmore Castle and rambling around the picturesque village of Merthyr Mawr. And even though Afan feels as though it is miles from anywhere urban, the bustling town of Swansea is just a short drive away – although the busy streets may come as something of a shock to the system after the natural, unspoiled beauty of Afan.

INFORMATION

STAY Discover the joys of glamping with a stay in a 5-m (18-ft) tipi, in the shadow of 18th-century Ogmore Castle. **Tipi Wales** (0845 409 0771; tipiwales.co.uk) combines nights under canvas with a full Welsh breakfast at the farmhouse tea room. Stay in a little more comfort at the **Tree Tops Guesthouse** (01639 812419; treetopsguesthouse.net) in Neath, which makes a great base for exploring the region. Or splurge on a weekend at the **Dragon Hotel** (01792 657100; dragon-hotel.co.uk) in Swansea, a great option for families, with a large pool and close access to the beach.

EAT Culinary sorts should pay their respects at **Patricks with Rooms** (01792 360199; patrickswithrooms.com), one of the region's most popular restaurants. No visit to Wales is complete without a meal at a classic Welsh pub; the **Colliers** (01639 643187; thecolliers.biz) is a family-run pub that does wonderful things with salt-marsh lamb. In Swansea, drop into the **Pump House** (01792 651080; pumphouseswansea.com), for excellent Welsh bangers and mash and glorious views across the harbour.

MORE INFO
afanforestpark.co.uk

GETTING THERE Leave the M4 at junction 40 and follow the brown signs to Afan.

OTHER GREAT CYCLING LOCATIONS
• Glentress, Scottish Borders (forestry.gov.uk/glentress)
• Grizedale, Cumbria (imba.org.uk)
• Fort William, Highland (ridefortwilliam.co.uk)

08 Walk Beneath the Blossom
BROGDALE, ENGLAND

Spend a spring weekend in the Garden of England, where the Kent soil gives bloom to apple, cherry, almond and plum orchards.

There is something uniquely beautiful about spring blossom. Perhaps it is the brevity of blossom season that makes it so moving; if the days bring blustery winds, the glorious pink and white cherry, apple and peach blossoms may only stay on the trees for a week or two before cascading to the ground. All the more reason, then, to make the most of this short burst of life-affirming colour with a visit to the National Fruit Collection at Brogdale Farm in Kent.

Brogdale boasts over 4,000 different varieties of fruit and nut trees, and the spring months when the apple, almond, pear, peach, cherry and plum trees come into flower are the best time to visit. It's a great place to bring the kids, with guided walks, plenty of opportunities to taste different types of fruit and nuts and a mini railway for all the family to ride on. The farm is located on the outskirts of the historic market town of Faversham, which makes a great base for exploring this often overlooked corner of Kent.

Faversham dates back to Roman times and is mentioned in the Domesday Book; but its more recent history is literally explosive. From the 1500s to the early 20th century it was the centre of the UK's gunpowder industry, and the town is steeped in its industrial heritage with 400 listed buildings and one of England's prettiest medieval streets, Abbey Street. For a glimpse of the town's premier industry, pop into Chart Gunpowder Mill (off Stonebridge Way), which was Faversham's first gunpowder factory, dating back to the 16th century, and is now an interesting museum.

But on a sunny spring day it is gardens, rather than museums, that are the big draw – and Kent is famous for them. Azaleas, rhododendrons and camellias blaze vibrant colours in gardens such as Mount Ephraim (mountephraimgardens.co.uk)

OPPOSITE: Visitors to the National Fruit Collection can admire the spectacular blossom on foot or take a tractor-trailer tour.

and Belmont House and Gardens (belmont-house.org). Belmont has been in the same family since 1801, and the elegant 18th-century house is open to visitors, alongside the rolling parkland and beautifully landscaped gardens.

The area around Faversham is also great walking country, with dozens of rambles of various lengths. From Faversham itself, the Two Creeks walk runs through the Thames Estuary, which used to be the known as the 'larder of London', due to the

RIGHT: Abbey Street in Faversham puts on a splendid floral display. BELOW: The gardens at Mount Ephraim were laid out in the early 1900s and substantially restored in the 1950s.

INFORMATION

STAY Make the most of the rolling countryside by staying in a country pub: the **White Horse** (01227 751343; whitehorsecanterbury.co.uk) at Boughton under Blean offers comfortable rooms above a cosy, traditional bar. Combine countryside with coast by staying at the **Hotel Continental** (01227 280280; hotelcontinental.co.uk) in Whitstable, a sleek and stylish beachfront address. Kids will adore staying on the farm at **Brenley Farmhouse** (01227 751203; brenley-farm.co.uk), while parents will love the spacious comfortable rooms and fabulous breakfasts.

EAT The **Dove** (01227 751360; shepherdneame.co.uk), in the village of Dargate, is renowned locally for its food and for the live music nights in the pretty garden. Combine a blow along Whitstable beach with a slap-up seafood supper at the **Crab and Winkle** (01227 779377; crabandwinklerestaurant.co.uk), which overlooks the town's fish market and serves up the catch of the day, fresh off the boat. Sip a glass of Kentish wine with a light lunch at **Woodrose Restaurant** (01227 751169; mountephraimgardens.co.uk), an atmospheric cafe housed in the former servants' quarters at Mount Ephraim House.

MORE INFO
brogdalecollections.co.uk

GETTING THERE Leave the M2 at Junction 6 and follow signs to Brogdale.

OTHER GREAT BLOSSOM SITES
• Westonbirt Arboretum, Gloucestershire (forestry.gov.uk/westonbirt)
• Vale of Evesham, Worcestershire (cotswolds.info)
• Batsford Arboretum, Gloucestershire (batsarb.co.uk)

countless ships and barges bound for the capital, carrying food, grain, hops and other materials. Alternatively, walk the Footsteps of Royalty and Romans trail, which takes in medieval buildings and historic sites, as well as Brogdale itself.

Mix rural rambles with a blast of sea air by heading up to the coast to Whitstable, which has cleaned up its act in recent years and mixes a rambling high street with some sleek hotels and restaurants. Stop for a drink right on the beach at the quirky Neptune pub or, if you're self-catering, visit the fish market for fresh seafood and the catch of the day – perfect for a traditional Kentish supper.

09 Visit Constable Country
DEDHAM, ENGLAND

Explore the beautiful Essex countryside and villages that inspired some of John Constable's most celebrated and best-loved landscape paintings.

'With all that lies on the banks of the Stour; those scenes made me a painter and I am grateful.' So said John Constable, who grew up in the small Essex village of Dedham in the late 18th century and went on to become arguably England's greatest landscape painter of all time. The landscapes of the Dedham Vale have remained relatively unchanged since Constable's time: sleepy villages and quiet hills that roll down to the banks of the river Stour, rich in wildlife and artistic heritage.

Dedham Vale is part of the Stour Valley, which sits right on the border between Suffolk and Essex and is famed for being the birthplace not just of Constable, but also Thomas Gainsborough, Paul Nash and Sir Alfred Munnings – who became president of the Royal Academy. The Alfred Munnings Museum in Dedham (siralfredmunnings. co.uk) was the artist's former home and has the largest collection of his work under one roof. The chance to look at some of his

beautiful landscapes, before walking in the very countryside he painted, is a memorable experience.

Dedham makes a great base for exploring this area of the country. The pretty high street is dotted with delis, gift shops and tea rooms and lined with elegant Georgian facades that often disguise buildings dating back to medieval times. Sherman's House is reputedly where John Constable attended school, and at the end of the high street the three-storey Arts and Crafts Centre is a great place to browse (and buy).

The nearby village of Flatford is a must-visit for any Constable enthusiast; the inspiration for many of his paintings, it's an easy walk across the water meadows from Dedham, and many of the views will be instantly recognizable from Constable's works. Pop into Bridge Cottage (nationaltrust.org.uk) in Flatford, which has an exhibition on Constable and offers

RIGHT: *Dedham's attractive high street.* BELOW: *Flatford Mill, owned by John Constable's father, features in many of the artist's paintings. The Field Studies Council runs residential art courses at the Mill – perfect for would-be Constables.*

guided tours around the village. From there, it's a gentle amble to the nearby village of East Bergholt, the birthplace of Constable.

Besides art, there is plenty more to discover in Dedham Vale. A designated Area of Outstanding Natural Beauty, the area is rich in wildlife – in spring it is possible to hear rare skylarks and chiffchaffs, or see hares boxing in the fields and badger cubs emerging from their lairs. The river Stour is home to otters and water voles, and there's plenty of opportunity to get out on the water, with regular boat trips from Flatford, and between Sudbury and Stour (riverstourtrust.org).

The lush and unspoiled Dedham Vale is about as far from the popular image of 'Essex' as it is possible to get. Although under an hour away from London there is a truly rural feel to the former wool towns and villages, and the countryside is latticed with ancient lanes and footpaths that make it easy to explore on foot, bike or horseback. The Painters' Trail is a 111-km (69-mile) circular route which links all the main artistic sites, but riding even just a short section is enough to see why these bucolically beautiful landscapes have provided such inspiration for artists over the centuries.

INFORMATION

STAY The **Sun Inn** (01206 323351; thesuninndedham.com) in Dedham is the perfect English pub: a low-beamed bar, cosy dining room serving up simple, well-prepared dishes and five comfortable rooms upstairs. For an elegant country escape, **Maison Talbooth** (01206 322367; milsomhotels.com) has 12 luxurious bedrooms, a state-of-the-art spa and Le Talbooth restaurant, idyllically situated on the banks of the Stour. **West Lodge** (01206 299808; westlodge.uk.com) offers B&B in a beautiful converted coach house, close to the village of East Bergholt.

EAT The tea room at **Bridge Cottage** (01206 298260; nationaltrust.org.uk) is the perfect spot on a warm spring day, with tables overlooking the river and wonderfully indulgent cream teas on offer. Whether for lunch, afternoon tea or supper, the location of the **Boat House Restaurant** (01206 323153; dedhamboathouse.co.uk) on the banks of the Stour is idyllic, and the food is pretty good too. The **Angel Inn** in nearby Stoke-by-Nayland (01206 263245) is a quaint country pub with a welcoming atmosphere and good food.

MORE INFO
dedhamvalestourvalley.org

GETTING THERE Dedham Vale lies on the A12, accessed from the A14 from the Midlands.

OTHER ARTISTIC AREAS
• St Ives, Cornwall (stives-cornwall.co.uk)
• The Lake District (golakes.co.uk)
• The Yorkshire Dales (yorkshire.com)

10 Picnic in the Park
REGENT'S PARK, LONDON

Soak up the scents and colours in Queen Mary's Rose Garden, spread a picnic blanket on the grass or snooze in a deckchair, as you spend a lazy day in the capital's loveliest park.

In a world where shop-bought roses often come with as much scent as a bowl of steam, the chance to walk through gardens of blooms, where the air is sweet with their natural perfume, is a reminder of how beautiful roses smell as well as look. The rose garden in London's Regent's Park is one of the most spectacular in the country and at its best in late spring, when over 400 different varieties of rose come into bloom.

Regent's Park was originally designed by William Nash for the Prince Regent, flanked by elegant mansions, many of which still stand today. Queen Mary's Gardens – home to the rose garden – was created in the 1930s, when the park was first opened to the general public. Nowadays, it's perfectly possible to spend an entire day in Regent's Park; take a boat out on the lake, have a snooze in one of the hireable deckchairs, stop for lunch at one of the

RIGHT: There are about 30,000 rose plants in Queen Mary's Rose Garden.

alfresco cafes and, if you've got the kids in tow, the tigers, giraffes, otters and penguins who all call London Zoo (zsl.org) home will keep them happily entertained for hours. Alternatively, the park is home to the capital's leading alfresco theatre (openairtheatre.org), with Shakespeare and child-orientated plays both on offer.

Regent's Park is helpfully situated between two of London's best – and most different – shopping experiences. Head south to the department stores and boutiques on Oxford Street, or north to the bohemian Camden Market (camdenlock.net), a kind of weekly mini Glastonbury, with an indoor craft market, foodie stalls and all the tie-dye you can

ABOVE: Queen Mary's Rose Garden.
BELOW: Quizzical giraffes at London Zoo.

INFORMATION

STAY Bust the budget with an indulgent stay at Gordon Ramsay's first hotel: **York and Albany** (020 7387 5700; gordonramsay.com/yorkandalbany/), a short walk from the park with a signature restaurant that does fabulous Sunday roasts. Sherlock Holmes fans should book the **Travelodge** (travelodge.co.uk) in Marylebone, a short walk from both the park and the famous sleuth's address on Baker Street. **Jury's Inn** (jurysinns.com) in Islington is an affordably priced, comfortable hotel just a short walk from the shops and restaurants on Upper Street.

EAT The **Garden Cafe** (020 7935 5729; companyofcooks.com) in the heart of the park has plenty of outdoor seating and serves up hearty seasonal food. A short walk north of the park lies bijou Primrose Hill, home to the **Engineer** (020 7722 0950; the-engineer.com), a fabulous gastropub that opens for slap-up breakfasts from 9 a.m. every day. For a gourmet picnic, pop into **Villandry** (020 7631 3131; villandry.com) on Great Portland Street, which specializes in French delicacies from croissants to charcuterie, with a restaurant alongside the deli.

MORE INFO royalparks.gov.uk

GETTING THERE Take the Tube – Regent's Park station (Bakerloo line), or walkable from Baker Street station (Bakerloo, Metropolitan, Circle) and Great Portland St station (Metropolitan, Circle).

OTHER SPECTACULAR ROSE GARDENS
• Sissinghurst, Kent (nationaltrust.org.uk)
• Drum Castle, Aberdeenshire (nts.org.uk)
• Castle Howard, Yorkshire (castlehoward.co.uk)

handle at the outdoor market situated along Camden Lock.

At the western end of the park lies Baker Street, a familiar name to all aficionados of Sir Arthur Conan Doyle's fictional sleuth, Sherlock Holmes. Today 221b Baker Street, the home of Holmes in the books, is the Sherlock Holmes Museum (sherlock-holmes.co.uk), with rooms kept as they would have been during the Victorian era of Doyle's books.

Further afield, there are a handful of London's 'villages' close to Regent's Park that all have their own character and feel. Hop a tube to Islington, and browse the antique stalls and market along Camden Passage, or jump on a bus up to Hampstead to see the city's rich and beautiful at play - and take a stroll on Hampstead Heath, the wildest of all London's green spaces. Within walking distance of the park lies Marylebone, a chic little area just a stone's throw from Oxford Street, but with a delightfully villagey feel and some great shops and restaurants.

The joy of a weekend in this area of London – combining the park with some lesser-known locations – is that it gives a glimpse of the capital away from the bright lights and hordes of tourists. On a warm spring day, with flowers in bloom, pavements dotted with restaurant tables and the diverse architecture glinting in the sunshine, it's no exaggeration to say that London really is one of the most beautiful cities in the world.

11 Drive the Romantic Road
COTSWOLDS, ENGLAND

Take the road less travelled and discover some of Gloucestershire's most picturesque villages on this tranquil back-roads tour.

Ah, England in the spring time: lambs gambolling in the fields, carpets of bluebells, tea and buns in sunlit tea shops, a babbling brook at the bottom of the garden. It may sound like the opening of a 1930s Enid Blyton novel, but this vision of England at its most, well, English, does still exist. The picturesque villages that dot the Cotswold hills, all thatched cottages and pristine village greens, make an idyllic weekend escape, with luxurious hotels, chic restaurants and cosy tea rooms all housed in warm, honey-coloured Cotswold stone.

The Romantic Road is a driving route put together by the local tourist board (download from cheltenham.info), with two sections taking in the southern and northern Cotswolds. First-time visitors to the area should drive the northern section, which

OPPOSITE: Stow-on-the-Wold is one of the Cotswolds' prettiest villages, with a high street lined with art galleries and gift shops.

takes in some of the most beautiful of all the villages. The drive can easily be done in a day, or over a weekend, with overnight stops in two or more villages.

One of the first places to visit on the northern route is the quirkily named Upper and Lower Slaughter. Although their name sounds as if it denotes a bloody history, in fact it simply comes from the old English 'slohtre', which means 'muddy place'. The Slaughters are anything but muddy places these days, instead offering a glimpse of England at the beginning of the 20th century; neither village has undergone any building work since 1906.

Bourton-on-the-Water is dominated by the river Windrush that flows through its heart, with six bridges spanning the two banks. Regularly voted the prettiest village in England, Bourton is a great place for families, with a model village to explore, and a Model Railway Exhibition (bourtonmodelrailway.co.uk), which has over 46 sq. m (500 sq. ft) of railway on show.

ABOVE: Chipping Campden was one of the most important of the medieval wool towns.

Moreton-in-Marsh and Chipping Campden, the most northerly of the Cotswold villages, have bustling high streets dotted with traditional shops, without a Starbucks in sight. There are some beautiful gardens to explore in this area of the Cotswolds that are at their most stunning in late spring: Batsford Arboretum (batsarb.co.uk), with carpets of bluebells and flaming azaleas and rhododendrons, and Hidcote (nationaltrust.org.uk), one of the country's great gardens, with its beautiful herbaceous borders.

Also on the northern route is the village of Broadway, home to the Lygon Arms, which has played host to both King Charles and Oliver Cromwell. Broadway has been documented as a settlement since 1900BC, and in more recent times became a favourite place for artists and writers such as Henry James and William Morris. It is the archetypal Cotswolds town: warm yellow stone glinting in the sunshine, a sleepy high street and a village green, lined with a mix of Tudor, Stuart and Georgian houses.

INFORMATION

STAY For the quintessential Cotswolds experience, stay at the **Cotswold House Hotel** (01386 840330; cotswoldhouse.com) in Chipping Campden, a beautiful Regency town house with luxury rooms and an elegant spa. The **Windy Ridge Estate** (01451 830465, windy-ridge.co.uk) in Moreton-in-Marsh offers the chance to stay in a beautiful Cotswold country house, at B&B prices. The **Lamb Inn** in Great Rissington is a traditional Cotswolds pub with a good choice of luxurious suites and simpler rooms, and a cosy bar and excellent restaurant beneath.

EAT For a really special meal, **Russell's** (01386 853555; russellsofbroadway.co.uk) in Broadway is one of the Cotswold's premier culinary addresses, serving up seasonal local food in Modern British dishes. After a blustery spring walk, settle in for lunch at the **Horse & Groom** (01451 830584; horseandgroom.uk.com) near Moreton-in-Marsh, where locally sourced meats make a fabulous roast lunch. For a classic Cotswolds tea room, drop into **Badger's Hall** tea rooms (01386 840839; badgershall.com) in Chipping Campden.

MORE INFO
the-cotswolds.org

GETTING THERE The starting point of the Romantic Road is Cheltenham, which lies on the A40 (leave the M5 at Junction 11).

OTHER ROMANTIC ROADS
• The Atlantic Highway, Cornwall (atlantic-highway.co.uk)
• Hardknott Pass, Cumbria (golakes.co.uk)
• The Loch Ness Monster Drive, Highland (visitscotland.com)

12 Stay in a Tree House
KELDY, ENGLAND

Return to childhood and experience Yorkshire's spectacular natural landscapes from a whole new perspective by spending a weekend in a luxury tree house.

There is something unique, and almost mystical, about the atmosphere of a forest. Perhaps it is the sense of life all around, but never quite visible: squirrels and birds in the trees, badgers and voles rustling through the undergrowth, the quick flash of a deer disappearing into waist-high ferns. The North York Moors National Park is often thought of as miles of empty moorland, but it also has lush forests which offer a wonderful sense of escape for a weekend break.

On the southernmost edge of the park, close to the market town of Pickering, lie great swathes of forest, with cabins dotted throughout, including luxury en suite apartments perched high up in the trees. Ideal for a family weekend away, there is plenty to do in the forest, with an excellent network of walking routes and mountain-bike trails, along with rock climbing and even the chance to fly a small aircraft. All

RIGHT: Everyone loves a tree house, especially when it has an en suite bathroom!

activities can be organized through Forest Holidays (0845 130 8225), and there is also a programme of Forest Ranger activities, including survival days and wildlife-watching evenings.

A short drive from Keldy lies Dalby Forest, which has some great play centres for younger children and a Go Ape (goape.co.uk) course, which offers the chance to climb, scramble and zip wire through the trees, with parts of the course reaching as high as 35m (115ft). If you're feeling lazy, there is also the 15-km (9-mile) Dalby Forest Drive, which winds through the

ABOVE: Some 32km (20 miles) east of Pickering is the Kilburn White Horse, which was carved into the hillside in 1857. INSET OPPOSITE: Dalby Forest offers over 64km (40 miles) of mountain-bike trails.

trees and gives the chance to explore the spectacular countryside – which dates back to the Ice Age – from behind the wheel. Dalby is well worth visiting at night too, as the dark skies are ideal for star-spotting, with regular 'star-watching' evening events.

But a stay in Keldy doesn't have to be all about rural pursuits. There are some

INFORMATION

STAY The Golden Oak Tree Houses at **Keldy Forest** (0845 130 8225; forestholidays.co.uk) offer the unique experience of a luxury stay amongst the tree canopy, deep in the forest. A little too rustic? **Stable Cottage** is a cosy cottage situated on the owner's farm on the outskirts of the village of Cropton – one of many available through Dales Holiday Cottages (0844 847 1340; dales-holiday-cottages. com **17 Burgate** (01751 473463; 17burgate.co.uk) in Pickering is a beautifully converted town house with luxury rooms and a cute walled garden.

EAT The **New Inn** (01751 417330; newinncropton.co.uk) at Cropton is a lovely pub with a brewery at the bottom of the garden and top-notch local food including Whitby crab and Yorkshire sausages. The **Treetops Restaurant** (01751 460454) at the Dalby Forest Visitor Centre offers home-made cakes and muffins, and lunch dishes that use herbs and veg grown in their own vegetable patch. The **Blackboard** (01653 668614; beansheafhotel.com/barRestaurant.html) is a great bet for families, with three different children's menus and free kids' activity packs.

MORE INFO
northyorkmoors.org.uk

GETTING THERE Turn off the A170 at the sign to Cropton, and look for the sign to Keldy Forest cabins after the New Inn pub in Cropton village.

OTHER TREE HOUSE STAYS
• The Tree House, Halse, Somerset (treehouseholidays.co.uk)
• Coates Castle, Fittleworth, Sussex (castlecottage.info)
• Deerpark, Cornwall (forestholidays.co.uk)

charming market towns nearby. Pickering has an agreeable bustle about it, particularly on market days. It also has a ruined 13th-century motte-and-bailey castle (englishheritage.org) and is the starting point for the spectacular North York Moors Railway (nymr.co.uk). 'Yorkshire's answer to the Orient Express' may be a slight exaggeration, but the NYMR does offer the chance to see the stunning countryside in serious style. The traditional steam trains are complete with wood-panelled carriages and conductor service, and run for 29km (18 miles) between Pickering and 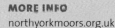 Grosmont, with the line carrying on to Whitby, and branching off west into the picturesque Esk Valley.

Slightly further afield, the beautiful town of York (visityork.org) is easily accessible for a day trip, or an afternoon's shopping. The iconic York Minster is one of Britain's most beautiful churches, but the real pleasure is simply strolling the cobbled streets and ancient alleyways, dipping into the individual boutiques and quirky shops. A stop for afternoon tea is a must, and there is nowhere better than Bettys (bettys.co.uk) – a classic slice of Yorkshire on a plate.

13 Go Island-hopping
THE INNER HEBRIDES, SCOTLAND

Ride the ferries between Mull, Tiree and Iona and discover the windswept beauty and unchanged way of life of Scotland's Western Isles.

The islands that make up the Inner Hebrides – including Mull, Coll, Tiree, Lismore and Kerrera, along with tiny isles such as Iona and Luing – are some of the most accessible of all Scotland's isles, yet they all share a feeling of wild remoteness that gives a true feeling of escape. The main islands are linked by regular ferries to the busy port of Oban, and it's easy to hop between the mainland and one or more of the islands for an unforgettable weekend.

The island of Mull makes an ideal base for a few days discovering the unchanged landscapes and way of life that give the Inner Hebrides such a particular feel. The

BELOW: Built as a fishing port in the late 18th century, Tobermory is a picture-postcard town with its brightly painted houses.

island's main town of Tobermory is famous for the brightly coloured houses that line the harbour front (the location for the TV series *Balamory*). Mull is particularly rich in wildlife, with minke whales, dolphins, porpoises and basking sharks all seen in its crystal-clear waters, while golden eagles can often be seen soaring overhead. Mull Magic (mullmagic.com) runs wildlife walks across the island, and also on Iona and Ulva.

From Mull it's just a five-minute hop to the tiny island of Iona, famous as the place where St Columba landed in AD563, bringing Christianity to Britain. Iona is rich in history and spirituality – although tiny, with just 90 residents, it is home to the ruins of an ancient nunnery, a restored medieval abbey and is the reputed burial ground of 48 Scottish kings. At just 5km (3 miles) long

and 2.4km (1½ miles) wide, it's easily possible to walk round the entire island in a day, and visit the nunnery and abbey – making it perfect for a day trip from Mull.

Tiree, the most westerly of the Inner Hebrides, enjoys more sunshine than almost anywhere else in the British Isles, thanks to the presence of the Gulf Stream. Both Tiree and Coll are famous for their stunning, 'white-sand' beaches – actually millions of tiny pieces of crushed shells. The tempestuous winds that often race across the islands make the beaches more of a draw for windsurfers than sunbathers, with the Tiree Wave Classic bringing the world's best windsurfers to the island every October.

Gardeners should cross the 18th-century humpback bridge that links the island of Seil to the mainland, and visit the stunning gardens of An Cala. In the spring months the gardens are at their most beautiful, with vibrant azaleas and Japanese cherries in full flower, while the formal garden at Ardmaddy Castle shows blooming rhododendrons and glorious formal borders. From Seil, hop across to Easdale, with its architecturally stunning arts and community centre and a sweet folk museum – before a quick ferry journey back to Mull, and another spectacular seafood supper.

ABOVE: From the 16th century onward Iona Abbey fell into ruin. Restoration, begun in 1902, has restored the abbey and its cloisters to their former glory. RIGHT: Traigh Feall is one of the many beautiful white-sand beaches on Coll.

INFORMATION

STAY Stay in a little piece of history at the **Bellachroy** (01688 400314; thebellachroy), the oldest inn on Mull, dating back to 1608. Slap-up seafood and cosy bedrooms make it a top choice. Live like a laird in one of the self-catering cottages and lodges on the **Glengorm Castle** estate (01688 302321; glengormcastle.co.uk), which has an excellent farm shop on site. The **Coll Hotel** (01879 230334; collhotel.com) on the island of Coll has a warm atmosphere, with six en suite rooms, an excellent restaurant and beautiful gardens.

EAT Eat fruit and vegetables fresh from the garden at **Ninth Wave** (01681 700757; ninthwave restaurant.co.uk) on Mull, along with seafood and meats from local fishermen and farms. **Martyrs Bay** (01681 700382; martyrsbay.co.uk) is the top choice on Iona, not least because it's the only pub on the island, but it has fabulous fresh seafood too. The unusually named **Elephant's End** (01879 220694; elephantsend.com) on Coll serves up home-made bread, cakes and pastries and local seafood and steaks.

MORE INFO visitscottishheartlands.com

GETTING THERE Oban lies at the end of the A85, which connects to the M90 via the A9.

OTHER SCOTTISH ISLAND GROUPS
- Orkney Isles (visitorkney.com)
- Shetland Isles (shetlandtourism.com)
- Summer Isles (summer-isles.com)

summer

Come rain or shine, we live to be outdoors in the summer months. The long sunlit days are when we truly show ourselves to be island people - our coastline comes alive with sailing regattas, beach parties and bucket-and-spade holidays, while weekends are dominated by festivals of all shapes and sizes. Eternal optimists, we plan alfresco theatre trips and evening picnics and when the rain pours down we simply smile and shrug and resign ourselves to the joys of the British summertime.

14 Punt Along the Cam
CAMBRIDGE, ENGLAND

Spend a quintessentially English day gliding past the elegant Cambridge colleges before taking afternoon tea beneath the apple trees at Granchester.

There's something ridiculously romantic about gliding along in a punt. Images of Sebastian Flyte clutching his teddy bear, Aloysius, of wicker hampers filled with champagne and strawberries and floppy-haired young men reciting Byron as they wobble precariously on the back of the boat. Ridiculously romantic, that is, as long as you are not having to do the punting yourself. Hefting a 3.6-m (12-foot pole) in and out of the river is not a relaxing pastime; far better to pay someone else for their trouble and simply lie back and enjoy the ride.

Fortunately, there are plenty of willing punters in Cambridge: impecunious students who happily spend their weekends propelling visitors up and down the Cam. Scudamores (scudamores.com) offer self-hire or chauffeured punts, but those in search of an indulgent afternoon should book a chauffeured punt and allow enough time to reach the Orchard Tea Garden at Granchester (orchard-grantchester.com), a couple of miles upriver from the city itself.

The Tea Gardens are a truly idyllic spot with a rich history, most famous as the former student lodgings of the renowned war poet Rupert Brooke. The owners of Orchard House took in student lodgers and in 1909 Brooke moved in. The Tea Garden was created when the students asked if they could take their tea beneath the blossoming fruit trees in the orchard, rather than on the lawn of the house, and as news spread of this tranquil bolt-hole, just slightly removed from the pressures of Cambridge life, so the gardens became a commercial concern.

Besides gliding along the river, the other way to approach the tea rooms is to walk the foot and cycle path, known as the 'Grantchester Grind' from Cambridge along the banks of the Cam. It's a couple of hours stroll, depending on your pace, but the terrain is flat, and if it's a hot day the Cam is coolly inviting for a quick dip.

OPPOSITE: The arms of Magdalene College, which was founded in the 16th century. BELOW: A visit to Cambridge is not complete without a punt trip along the Backs, a mile-long stretch of the river Cam that takes in eight colleges and nine bridges.

INFORMATION

STAY The **Hotel du Vin** (01223 227330; hotelduvin.com) is the city's most stylish address, with a buzzy brasserie, a cosy bar and stylish double rooms that manage to pair minimalism with luxury. To really experience Cambridge, the best way is to actually stay in college: in student vacations, 12 of the **Cambridge colleges** offer B&B, giving a unique insight into student life (cambridgerooms.co.uk). Combine urban with rural pleasures by staying outside of town on the **Cambridge Caravanning & Camping Club Site** (01223 841185), which has excellent facilities.

EAT Committed carnivores will love the **Cambridge Chop House** (01223 359506; cambridgechophouse.co.uk); hefty slabs of meat, rich gravy and home-made sausages are not for the faint-hearted. The **Kingston Arms** (01223 319414; kingston-arms.co.uk) is a cosy gastropub with reassuringly un-gastro prices. Keep the traditional feel with a visit to **Aunties Tea Shop** (1 St Mary's Passage, auntiesteashop.co.uk) for tea and home-made scones.

GETTING THERE Leave the M11 at Junction 12 and take the A603 east towards Cambridge.

MORE INFO visitcambridge.org

OTHER PLACES TO PUNT
• Discover Oxford by punting along the Cherwell (cherwellboathouse.co.uk).
• Glide along the river Stour in Canterbury (canterburypunting.co.uk).
• See the beautiful city of Bath from another perspective (bathboating.co.uk).

A punt along the river makes a welcome break from the sightseeing that is all part of a trip to one of Britain's most beautiful cities. The Cambridge colleges are open to visitors (apart from in May when some may be closed due to examinations) but they do charge; a small price to pay, however, for strolling in the imposing grounds of King's College (kings.cam.ac.uk), where Charles Darwin once studied.

OPPOSITE: Clare Bridge gives access to the main court of Clare College (founded in 1326). INSET ABOVE: The 19th-century Gothic New Court of St John's College (founded in 1511).

Cambridge is a city dominated by academia, but its student population means that it retains a vibrant, fun feel. Combine a visit to the Fitzwilliam Museum (fitzwilliam.cam.ac.uk) – crammed full with exhibits from ancient Egypt, Rome and the Near East – with a stroll through the stunning Botanic Gardens (botanic.cam.ac.uk), where plants from all over the world are dotted through 16ha (40 acres) of lushly beautiful gardens. Heritage, architecture, nightlife – Cambridge has it all – and yet there is nothing that quite beats sitting in a deckchair beneath the apple trees in Grantchester, sipping tea and tucking into scones piled high with jam and cream. Summer perfection.

15 Watch the Gig Racing
SCILLY ISLES, ENGLAND

Join the locals for their highly competitive weekly rowing competitions that take place in the waters between Cornwall's unique island hideaways.

There is something very special about the Isles of Scilly. Arrive by air and the islands appear suddenly out of the vast Atlantic Ocean; seemingly little more than white-fringed rocks, gradually increasing in size as the plane draws near. Their isolated location – 96km (60 miles) south-west of the southernmost tip of the Cornish coast – gives the island community a close-knit sense of independence. The Scillies may be part of Cornwall, England and Britain – but those who live there are Scillonian before anything else.

However, in spite of their isolation, tourism has long made its way to the islands, by sea and air, and most islanders make their income from the small businesses dotted across the archipelago – cosy B&Bs, tranquil campsites, village shops where the staff know everyone's name. It's a place that seems to embody old-fashioned values – tradition, community and a warm welcome to visitors.

What's surprising about the Scillies is the diversity of the islands. Each of the five inhabited islands have a different atmosphere – most visitors become life-long advocates of one particular style: the wild, isolated feel of Bryher, the picture-book prettiness of Tresco, the peace and tranquillity of St Agnes. Happily it's easy to visit all of the islands on a week's holiday; inter-island ferries run regularly, although it's worth keeping an eye on the tide times as it's quite easy to get stranded on the wrong island if you miss the last boat of the day.

Gig racing is an ideal way to get an insight into real Scillonian culture, and is the main sport on the islands. Gigs are 9.7-m (32-ft) wooden rowing boats – some of which are over 100 years old – with six single-oar positions and a cox. Every week there are inter-island races – Wednesday evenings for women and Friday for men.

OPPOSITE: It is possible to walk from St Agnes to Gugh Island at low tide.

INFORMATION

STAY If money is no object book into the **Hell Bay Hotel** (01720 422947; hellbay.co.uk), an outpost of luxury on wild, unkempt Bryher, with light, cosy rooms and a restaurant specializing in local fish dishes. Go back to nature at **Troytown Farm** (01720 422360; troytown.co.uk) on St Agnes, where you can pitch your own tent or camp in a pre-erected bell tent (sleeps four). The **Flying Boat Club** on Tresco is a collection of luxury self-catering cottages with all mod cons and wonderful views across to Bryher.

INSET: Gig racers vie for position.

EAT The **New Inn** (tresco.co.uk/stay/new-inn) on Tresco is a long-term Scillonian favourite, serving up fabulous fish dishes made from the morning's catch. Treat yourself to juicy St Agnes lobster at the **High Tide** seafood restaurant (01720 432869; hightide-seafood.com), where much of the food is produced on the islands. The **Dairy Cafe** on St Mary's is an ideal spot for a light lunch or a slice of home-made cake.

GETTING THERE *Scillonian III* sails six days a week, March to October, from Penzance to St Mary's. Skybus operate flights from five airports in the south west. To book either: 0845 710 5555; islesofscilly-travel.co.uk.

MORE INFO simplyscilly.co.uk

OTHER PLACES TO WATCH SAILING RACES
- Cowes Week, Isle of Wight (cowes.co.uk)
- Henley Regatta (hrr.co.uk)
- Whitby Regatta (whitbyregatta.co.uk)

Visitors can cheer on the teams and watch the – highly competitive – races from viewing boats that follow the gigs.

The weekly races are just one way in which these scattered islands are dominated by the sea. Whole mornings can be spent sitting on the beach watching the endless deliveries, the small passenger ferries and private boats all making their way across the shallow waters. Fishermen are well catered for, as the waters are rich in pollack, conger eels and even blue shark; try Scilly Fishing (scillyfishing.co.uk) for reef and shark fishing, as well as birdwatching trips.

No visit to the Scillies is complete without a visit to the stunning Abbey Gardens. Warmed by the jet stream that gives the Scillies their warm microclimate, the gardens are home to over 20,000 plants – many of which cannot be grown anywhere else in the UK. The carefully landscaped beds step up a hillside, and to sit at the top on a clear summer's day gives breathtaking views over the lush gardens to the sparkling sea beyond. The only places to beat the gardens are the beaches themselves: white-sand, undeveloped, utterly beautiful. If only the sea wasn't quite so cold …

16 Raise a Glass
SOUTH DOWNS, ENGLAND

Discover a taste for English wine on a tour of the vineyards springing up across the chalky soil of the Sussex countryside, home to Britain's newest national park.

Got something to celebrate? Or just love a glass of something sparkling? Well, forget heading across the Channel and instead point the car towards the bucolic South Downs, home to some award-winning sparkling wines and an increasingly vibrant wine industry. Sound a little unbelievable? In fact the chalky soil of the Downs is exactly the same as that which lies beneath France's champagne region – and our warmer summers are helping to produce a fine selection of sparkling wines.

BELOW: Sunshine, blue skies and grapes on the vine – yes, you are in Sussex, on the South Downs, not southern France!

These days, it's possible to spend a weekend popping in and out of vineyards for tastings and buying a bottle or two, just as British visitors have been doing in the Loire region of France for years. Start at Bookers Vineyard (bookersvineyard.co.uk) in Bolney, just north of Brighton, which has been operating for almost 40 years. The 9-ha (22-acre) vineyard is open daily for wine sales, and tours and tastings can be arranged (01444 881894).

A must-visit is the Ridgeview Wine Estate (ridgeview.co.uk) in Ditchling, which won the Decanter award for best sparkling wine in the world in 2010. The 12-ha (30-acre) estate has 'open to all' tasting dates (phone to check) or will offer tastings and tours for groups of eight or more. Don't miss the wonderfully named Breaky Bottom (breakybottom.co.uk) vineyard, one of the oldest in the country, with vines planted in 1974. Famous for its award-winning Seyval Blanc grape variety, the best buy is the sparkling 'Methode Champenoise Sparkling Brut'. Breaky Bottom is also handily placed for a visit to the pretty market town of Lewes, famed for having its own currency, the 'Lewes pound'.

The beauty of this area of the Downs is that you can mix rural (and vinicular) pleasures with the rather more urban pleasures of Brighton. Once somewhat down at heel, the town has had a facelift in recent years and on a sunny day the

BELOW: *Stopham Vineyard near Pulborough was planted in 2007, inspired by the white wines from Alsace. INSET OPPOSITE: The North Laine, Brighton, is a vibrant bohemian area boasting the largest selection of independent retailers on the South Coast.*

INFORMATION

STAY The **Bull** (01273 843147, thebullditchling.com) at Ditchling is a classic country pub – timber beams, log fires and cosy leather sofas – with four sleek rooms upstairs. The food is pretty good too. If you want to mix rural pleasures with some seaside fun, the **Neo** (01273 711104; neohotel.com) has nine sexy bedrooms in a fantastic central location in Brighton. If the weather is good, the South Downs are perfect camping territory; the beautiful, back-to-basics site at **Blackberry Wood** (01273 890035; blackberrywood.com) is the best in the county.

EAT East Chiltington's **Jolly Sportsman** (01273 890400; thejollysportsman.com) is a classic gastropub with a beautiful garden, serving up locally sourced food from simple plates of charcuterie to full three-course suppers. On a sunny day in Brighton there's no better place for an indulgent lunch than **Due South** (01273 821218; duesouth.co.uk), right on the beach, with lip-smacking fresh fish and Sussex wines on the wine list. **Limes of Lindfield** (01444 487858; limesoflindfield.co.uk) is a jolly bistro on Lindfield's picturesque high street that serves up classic dishes and sumptuous puds.

GETTING THERE The A23 heads straight to Brighton, with signs to surrounding villages and vineyards.

MORE INFO visitsussex.org

OTHER VINEYARDS
• Denbies, Dorking, Surrey (denbies.co.uk)
• Three Choirs Vineyard, Gloucestershire (three-choirs-vineyards.co.uk)
• Ancre Hill Vineyard, Monmouth (ancrehillestates.co.uk)

---

beachfront promenade is lined with restaurants and bars that offer plenty of space outside to sit and soak up the seaside atmosphere. The town itself offers great shopping and strolling potential – most famously the Lanes, a cluster of alleyways that once ran between fishermen's houses. Now the Lanes are lined with galleries, jewellery shops, boutiques and cafes and are perfect for browsing.

The Lanes can get very crowded; to escape the hordes head away from the sea to the North Laine area – where a criss-cross of pedestrian streets mixes vintage shops with quirky cafes and cosy pubs. Should you feel the need for chain stores and mainstream shopping, Churchill Square has all the familiar names, but it has none of the charm of Brighton's more bohemian areas. Head east along the dramatic coast road and visit the picturesque villages of Alfriston and Rottingdean, or take a walk along the beaches that lie beneath the sheer cliffs. All are perfect spots for a blissful summer picnic – with a glass or two of local Sussex wine, naturally.

17 Watch a Well Dressing
BAKEWELL, ENGLAND

Experience one of Derbyshire's longest-held traditions, and join the colourful community-based celebrations that give thanks for the clean waters of local springs.

However futuristic parts of our society seem to become, England is still a country that is rich in tradition – and pegging a weekend break around some sort of rural festivity can make it really memorable. The Well Dressing festivities that take place around Derbyshire in late spring and summer are a great insight into village life: local wells and springs are adorned with intricate flower displays that depict religious or historic events.

Well dressing has a somewhat blurred history; some believe that the practice dates back to the mid-14th century, when England was ravaged by the Black Death. Villages in Derbyshire that were untouched by the plague put it down to their clean water supply, and gave thanks by 'dressing' the wells. Others believe that the tradition is much older and dates back to pagan times, as part of ancient spring fertility rites.

However the tradition began, it is alive and well in Derbyshire, with villages such as Eyam and Tissington creating particularly spectacular 'dressings'. Frequently the whole village takes part in creating the image, which involves thousands of petals placed on a wet clay board. There is usually a procession and a ceremony to bless the well, which often kicks off several days of festivities, including live music and morris dancing.

Many of the villages are too small to offer much in the way of accommodation, but the town of Bakewell makes a great base for exploring the spectacular Peaks countryside. The town is most famous for the almond and jam tart that bears its name (called a 'pudding' in Bakewell itself) and three shops in the town claim to have the original recipe, which was created accidentally in the 18th century at the Rutland Arms. The town is named after its wells (two of which still survive), and Bakewell celebrates its well dressing festival every June.

OPPOSITE ABOVE LEFT: Bakewell. ABOVE RIGHT: The market town of Wirksworth. BELOW: Spectacular well dressing created in Eyam.

Eyam

A Caring and Sharing village

INFORMATION

STAY The **Rutland Arms Hotel** (01629 812812; rutlandarmsbakewell.co.uk) has been open for business since 1804, and offers luxurious accommodation in the heart of Bakewell (it's also the birthplace of the Bakewell 'pudding'.) A few minutes walk out of town, **Castle Hill Farmhouse** (01629 813168; castlehillfarmhouse.co.uk) is a delightful B&B, in a cosy 17th-century farmhouse with a picturesque cottage garden. **Greenhills Holiday Park** (01629 813052; greenhillsholidaypark. co.uk) is a great budget option, with static vans and caravan and camping pitches, along with play areas for the kids.

EAT You can't visit Bakewell and not have a slice of the famous tart; the **Bakewell Pudding Shop** (01629 812193; bakewellpuddingshop.co.uk) is a cosy shop and cafe where you can also buy tarts to take away. For a classic pub lunch, the **Farmyard Inn** (01629 636221; farmyardinn.co.uk) is a short drive away in the village of Youlgreave. For an elegant dinner, **Piedaniels** (01629 812687; piedaniels-restaurant.com) offers modern French cooking in stylish surroundings, and an excellently priced set lunch.

MORE INFO peakdistrict.gov.uk

GETTING THERE Leave the M1 at junction 29, and follow the A617 to Chesterfield and then the A619 to Bakewell.

OTHER WELL DRESSING FESTIVALS
• Malvern, Worcestershire (visitworcestershire.org)
• Buxton, Derbyshire (buxtonwelldressing.co.uk)
• Newborough, Staffordshire (enjoystaffordshire.com)

The town dates back to Roman times, although most of the architecture dates to the 19th century, when the town was almost entirely rebuilt due to new-found prosperity brought about by the new corn mills. The town has one of the oldest markets in the area, dating back to the late 13th century, and livestock markets are still held every Monday. There are some lovely walks from the centre of the town. Head downstream along the river Wye and the walk takes in a beautiful 16th-century manor house and bridge, as well as Arkwright's Mill, which brought such prosperity to the town. The Bakewell Visitor Centre in the old Market Hall has plenty of information on local walks, rides and sights.

Although a visit to the Peaks is all about exploring the countryside, there is one visitor attraction that shouldn't be missed: Chatsworth House (chatsworth.org), one of England's most stunning stately houses. Home to an amazing private art collection, and instantly recognisable from films such as *Pride and Prejudice*, Chatsworth also has a beautiful 42-ha (105-acre) garden, and a farmyard and playground area that the kids will love.

18 Canoe the Wye River
MONMOUTH, WALES

Glide past the sleepy villages and ruined castles of Monmouthshire as you paddle your canoe along the tranquil waters of the Wye River.

On a hot summer's day there is no better place to be than on the water, gliding gently along in a canoe, with blue skies above and clear water below. Britain is latticed with tranquil and picturesque rivers, and one of the most beautiful is the Wye, which begins high up in the Welsh mountains at Plynlimon and flows through stunning Welsh countryside before meeting the Severn Estuary near Chepstow, some 215km (134 miles) later.

The Wye River is one of the richest in the whole of the country – in fish, in history and in the activities that it offers. One of the

BELOW: The famous view from Symonds Yat Rock, 120m (394ft) above the river Wye.

most beautiful stretches is from Goodrich Castle, passing the charming county town of Monmouth before flowing into the stunning Wye Valley and dramatic forest landscapes around Symonds Yat. Monmouth Canoe & Activity Centre (monmouthcanoe.co.uk) offers half-day or full-day trips, with a choice of routes up to 160km (100 miles). Although stretches of the river are suitable for novices and families, as the river heads towards Chepstow it becomes increasingly tidal and the stretch south of Tintern Abbey must always be done with a guide.

Besides messing about on the river, there is much to be explored in and around

ABOVE: What could be more peaceful than paddling gently down the river in a canoe? INSET OPPOSITE: The ruins of 12th-century Goodrich Castle.

Monmouth. All too often the border country is overlooked as people head deeper into Wales, and yet the countryside around the Wye Valley has a special beauty. The town itself is a rare find: a bustling high street where small, independent shops still flourish – and there is not a Starbucks or McDonalds to be seen. Pack a picnic and head up to the Kymin, a two-storey, circular banqueting house dedicated to the glories of the Royal Navy. Situated on top of a hill, there is a

INFORMATION

STAY In the heart of the pretty market town of Monmouth, **Bistro Prego** (01600 712600; pregomonmouth.co.uk) has eight neat en suite rooms above a buzzy brasserie; doubles from £60 B&B. **Steppes Farm Cottages** (01600 775424; steppesfarmcottages.co.uk) are ideal for a slice of rural life; 3km (2 miles) outside Monmouth these converted farm cottages come with all mod cons. To really experience the beauty of the countryside, camp, surrounded by lush woodland, at **Doward Park** (01600 890438; dowardpark.co.uk) near Symonds Yat.

EAT The **Ostrich** (01594 833260; theostrichinn.com) at Newland is a classic country pub: cosy bar, pretty garden and a menu of robust pub dishes that are all cooked with real flair. Indulge in a hearty lunch or tea and cake at **Goodrich Castle Tearoom** (english-heritage.org.uk), where everything is locally sourced and home made. Pair a visit to Raglan Castle with lunch at the **Cripple Creek Inn** (01291 690256; thecripplecreek.com), where local lamb and steaks are served up alongside good veggie options.

GETTING THERE Monmouth lies on the A40.

MORE INFO visitwyevalley.com

OTHER GREAT CANOEING RIVERS
• The river Thames, London (visitthames.co.uk)
• The river Spey, Scotland (sourceadventure.co.uk)
• The river Dart, Devon (canoeadventures.co.uk)

croquet set to hire, and the Offa's Dyke Path runs through the Kymin's grounds.

The whole of the Wye Valley and surrounding countryside is steeped in history, with ancient churches that sheltered the Knights Templar and spectacular ruined castles. Goodrich – one of the starting points for a canoe trip – is a spectacular ruin that dates back to the 11th century, while Raglan (cadw.wales.gov.uk) – a short drive south of Monmouth – is an impressive 15th-century castle with the state apartments and the Great Tower all still relatively intact.

The ideal weekend in this area is a day on the river plus a day exploring on foot. There are fantastic walks of all lengths in the area – the Wye Valley Walk follows the river from its source, but there are some lovely short stretches that can be done between Monmouth and Chepstow. Walk along the banks of the river from Symonds Yat, and reward yourself with a pint at the Saracen's Head on your return. Alternatively, follow the route from Redbrook up to Newland and the Cathedral in the Forest. Details of local walks can be obtained from the tourist information centre in Monmouth.

Of course on a hot summer's day the best activity of all is to combine a walk and the Wye – a gentle stroll beside the water and a long snooze in the shade on the banks of the river.

19

A Whizz-bang Weekend
PLYMOUTH, ENGLAND

Don't wait for Guy Fawkes Night; head to the Devon coast for the spectacular colour and sound effects of the National Fireworks Championships, held over two nights.

Who doesn't love a firework display? The only problem is that most of us have to wait for winter to get our pyrotechnic kicks – either on 5 November or watching the New Year fireworks on TV. One weekend every summer, however, the skies above the West Country city of Plymouth are lit up with a spectacular series of displays, as the best firework companies across the country compete to win the British Fireworks Championship (britishfireworks.co.uk). Over two nights, six companies each put on a display, with thousands of people gathering along the harbourfront to watch the explosions of colour above the English Channel.

The Fireworks Championship is just one reason to visit a city that is currently re-inventing itself as a vibrant holiday destination and host venue for the Olympics. At the heart of the city's redevelopment is the historic 16-km (10-mile) waterfront, which encompasses sites such as the Barbican area

(plymouthbarbican.com), from where Sir Francis Drake and the Pilgrim Fathers set sail, and the vibrant Victorian promenade lined with cafes and restaurants.

Plymouth is defined by its maritime history; one of the most iconic places in the city is Plymouth Hoe, where Sir Francis Drake famously played his game of bowls before defeating the Spanish Armada. But it's a modern city too, with the country's largest aquarium (national-aquarium.co.uk) – containing 50 tanks, home to sharks, octopus and rays – and interactive displays and hands-on exhibits at the impressive Mayflower Exhibition, which charts the famous expeditions that began in the city.

Plymouth also makes a great base for exploring the surrounding countryside and picturesque fishing villages that dot this area of the coast. Take the chain ferry across to Torpoint and head south to the pretty linked

OPPOSITE: Spectacular firework displays light up the skies above Plymouth.

villages of Kingsand and Cawsand: two higgledy-piggledy clutches of cottages, shops and cafes that open out onto small curved bays. It's an ideal spot for an afternoon by the sea, but beware – the waters are icy cold. Inland, the beautiful landscapes of the Dartmoor National Park are under half an hour's drive away.

If swimming – even in the height of summer – sounds a little hard-core, then the other way to explore the coast is on foot. The South West Coast Path (southwestcoast path.com) takes in the Plymouth waterfront,

BELOW LEFT: Ray display at the National Aquarium. BELOW RIGHT: Cawsand village. INSET OPPOSITE: Smeaton's Tower offers wonderful views of Plymouth Sound. OPPOSITE BOTTOM: Plymouth's historic coastline.

and there are some spectacular short walks close to the city, including the 11-km (7-mile) Forts and Castles of Plymouth Sound walk, which takes in the 17th-century citadel.

Of course no one should visit this most maritime of towns without setting sail on the seas that have witnessed the beginning of truly historic journeys. Plymouth Boat Trips (plymoutboattrips.co.uk) offers a variety of ways to get out on the water, from fishing trips to cruises around the historic dockyards, and small passenger ferries that run over to Kingsand and Cawsand. Alternatively, for something a little more thrilling, Devon Powerboating (devonpower boating.co.uk) offers powerboat and jet-ski rides that whisk through the Plymouth Sound at breakneck speed.

INFORMATION

STAY For a gastro-break, book into **St Elizabeths** (01752 344840; stelizabeths.co.uk), an elegant restaurant with rooms in a beautiful Georgian manor house in nearby Plympton. Stay across the water in the picturesque village of Kingsand. **Chough Cottage** sleeps up to six with lovely sea views; through Helpful Holidays (01647 433593; helpfulholidays.com – ref R46). **Seabreezes** (01752 667205; plymouth-bedandbreakfast. co.uk) is a luxury guesthouse with fluffy robes, plasma TVs and DVD players in the chic rooms, located right in the heart of the city.

EAT The **Barbican Kitchen** (01752 604448; barbicankitchen.com) is spectacularly located in the Plymouth Gin Distillery – where the Pilgrim Fathers spent their final night before heading for the New World. Dishes are simple, tasty and well prepared. For a good-value meal, the **Mission** (01752 229955; themissionplymouth.com) serves up classic bistro meals and nibbles, along with excellent cocktails. Head out of the city for a relaxing lunch in the countryside at the **Rose & Crown** (01752 880223; theroseandcrown.co.uk), an award-winning pub that offers elegant food in the restaurant and well-kept beers in the cosy bar.

GETTING THERE The A38 runs through Plymouth.

MORE INFO visitplymouth.co.uk

OTHER FANTASTIC FIREWORKS
• The Lord Mayor's Fireworks, London (lordmayorsshow.org)
• New Year's Eve, Edinburgh (edinburghshogmanay.com)
• Sparks in the Park, Cardiff (visitcardiff.com)

20 Celebrate Midsummer
UNST, SCOTLAND

Make the most of the long summer evenings with a weekend on the Shetland island of Unst – the northernmost tip of Great Britain.

Head to the northern tip of the island of Unst and you have officially reached the end of Great Britain; beyond it lies the pounding sea, stretching all the way up to the Arctic Circle. It's easy to imagine Unst as a windswept, bleak place, but in fact this 19 by 13km (12 by 8 mile) island is spectacularly beautiful, and rich in culture and heritage.

However, don't come to Unst expecting boutique hotels and Wi-Fi connection in your bedroom. This is an island dominated by nature and history, and there is an immense amount of both to explore. It's worth dipping into the Unst Heritage Centre, to get a feel for the place and how life is lived on the island – and the industries through which islanders make their living: crafting, fishing, quarrying and, of course, tourism.

Unst is a great place to go with children, because there are endless opportunities for adventuring and exploring, scrambling over ruins and running along beaches. Muness Castle (undiscoveredscotland.co.uk) is an atmospheric ruin dating back to the 16th century, while the Muckle Flugga Lighthouse is spectacularly perched on rocks at the northernmost tip of the island. The lighthouse was built by Thomas and David Stevenson – father and uncle of the author Robert Louis Stevenson – and there are those who believe that *Treasure Island* was based on the island of Unst. The best way to see it is on a boat trip: Muckle Flugga Charters (muckleflugga.co.uk) offer sightseeing trips around the area, as well as angling and diving days.

Kids will also love the chance to meet real-life Vikings, at Viking Unst (vikingshetland.com), a living history project. Unst was one of the first landfalls for Viking warriors and there are the remains of over 30 longhouses on the island. In the summer months, living history recreations

OPPOSITE: Perfect for walking, exploring tidal areas, paddling or lazing in the long days of sunshine.

frenzied pace of life on the British mainland. Whether you choose to explore by bike, on foot or by boat there is always something to see: ancient stone circles, clusters of birds, mysterious standing stones. And in summer, you have the most amount of time to do it; Shetlanders call it the 'Simmer Dim', because it never truly gets dark. The long days and dusky nights all add to the sense of mysticism and peace that defines this truly unique island.

LEFT: Puffins come ashore to nest from mid-April to early August. BELOW: Muckle Flugga Lighthouse. OPPOSITE: Gannets whiten the rocks at Muckle Flugga.

take place at a seasonal Viking camp, complete with a replica Viking longship.

The island is also a paradise for wildlife lovers with two nature reserves – Hermaness and the Keen of Hamar, home to dramatic landscapes of sheer cliffs and stretches of white sand beach. Hermaness is home to 15 different breeding species, including gannets, puffins and fulmars, while otters can often be seen all around the island. Dolphins and whales can sometimes be seen off the north coast in the summer months, Shetland ponies wander freely and there are also several species of orchid that flower naturally on the island.

The real joy of Unst is the tranquillity, slow pace and sense of distance from the

INFORMATION

STAY The **Baltasound Hotel** (01957 711334; baltasound-hotel.shetland.co.uk), Britain's most northerly hotel, has simple but comfortable rooms and a warm, informal welcome. The **Creek** (01957 711352; creekcrofthouse.co.uk) is a traditional croft house, sleeping up to four, with stunning views across Haroldswick Bay and excellent self-catering facilities. **Saxavord Resort** (01957 711711; saxavord.com) combines hostel and self-catering facilities with a lively on-site bar and restaurant.

EAT Non-residents can try some of the local Shetland produce at the **Saxavord** restaurant (as above) – renowned for its excellent seafood. **Springers**, the bar at the Baltasound Hotel (as above), offers lunch and supper for non-residents, as well as a takeaway service. If you're self-catering, the **Skibhoul Stores** in Baltasound has a good choice of food, freshly baked bread and is also licensed. There's an excellent farmers' market on the last Saturday of each month, a great chance to pick up some freshly caught seafood.

GETTING THERE Daily flights from Scotland's airports land at Sumburgh Airport, from where it is a magnificent drive via ferry to Unst. Alternatively, take the car ferry to Lerwick from Aberdeen.

MORE INFO unst.org

OTHER GREAT LOCATIONS ON THE LONGEST DAY
- Stonehenge, Wiltshire (stonehenge.co.uk)
- Thurso, Highland (undiscoveredscotland.co.uk)
- Holy Island, Northumberland (lindisfarne.org.uk)

21 Love the Lakes
WASTWATER, ENGLAND

Escape the crowds that flock to the Lake District in summer and discover the tranquil beauty of the countryside around Wasdale in Cumbria's quietest corner.

Pictures of the Lake District always show tranquil hills and dramatic landscapes, free of crowds and blissfully peaceful – but in the summer months this is often far from the case, as holidaymakers in their thousands flock to Windermere and Coniston. Wastwater, however, and the surrounding area of Wasdale, remain relatively untouched by the tourist hordes, due to their relative inaccessibility, and on a hot August day the peaks of Scafell Pike and Pillar, reflected in the crystal waters of Wastwater, are spectacularly beautiful.

Although a small area, Wasdale is defined by superlatives – Scafell Pike is the highest mountain in England and Wastwater is the deepest lake. It's also home to the smallest church in the country, St Olaf's, which must rank as one of the most peaceful places too. The roof trusses allegedly came from Viking ships. Although remote, Wasdale can be reached by car; the road comes to an end at Wasdale Head, which is

the starting point for those wanting to climb the challenging peaks in the area.

Even for experienced walkers, some of the hikes can be seriously taxing, and it's always a good idea to consider hiring a guide for the afternoon or day. Lake District Guiding (lake-district-guiding.co.uk) offers walks for all levels of fitness and experience, and can put together itineraries for any length of time from a few hours to a few days. For a full-on Lakes experience, Felltreks (felltrek.co.uk) offers hikes up Scafell Pike and Pillar.

As Wasdale is on the western side of the Lakes, it makes the perfect base for exploring the little-known Cumbrian coast. Even on a hot summer's day the stretches of beach along the Cumbrian coast remain relatively quiet, and the small town of St Bees is a great choice for a family day by the sea. The town has a spectacular beach, which stretches for a mile, with plenty of sand and a gently sloping shoreline which is

RIGHT: Wasdale Head Inn is renowned as the perfect base for Lakeland climbers. BELOW: Views of the tranquil waters of Wastwater and its surrounding peaks have inspired the imaginations of artists, writers, and climbers for centuries.

ideal for young children. Alongside the beach, the town is home to the impressive ruined priory of St Mary and St Bega, which dates back over 1,000 years.

There is also a spectacular walk up onto St Bees Head – a dramatic red sandstone bluff that reaches up to 91m (300ft). A great spot for twitchers, as there is an RSPB reserve on the headland that is home to the only colony of black guillemots in England, and there are observation points to watch the puffins, terns and other seabirds. At nesting times, the skies are full of wheeling kittiwakes, gulls and razorbills.

For a little more life, the elegant Georgian town of Whitehaven is a short drive away, with a bustling marina and a lively seaside atmosphere that is a world away from the silence of Wasdale. Even though it is a sizeable town it retains the slightly undiscovered feel that makes the Western Lakes so special – a hidden corner of one of Britain's most visited regions – the holy grail of a weekend away.

INFORMATION

STAY Famous as the birthplace of climbing, the **Wasdale Head Inn** (019467 26229; wasdale.com) is one of the most remote places to stay in Britain, with comfy bedrooms and self-catering apartments that are just the ticket after a long day's walking. The **YHA Wastwater** (0845 371 9350; yha.org.uk) is a stunning, half-timbered country house that dates back to the early 19th century, offering rooms sleeping from four to ten. Surrounded by 85ha (210 acres) of farmland, **Shepherds Views Holidays** (019467 299907; shepherdsviews.co.uk) offers camping and caravanning pitches and self-catering cottages.

EAT The **Strands Inn & Brewery** (01946 726 237; strandshotel.com) has its own microbrewery on the premises, and offers lunch and dinners that specialize in using local ingredients. There are also cosy rooms available. The **Dining Room** at the Wasdale Head Inn (as before) has an old-fashioned elegance and the kind of food that sets you up for a day's mountaineering. The **Woodlands Tea Room** (santonbridge.co.uk) is a short drive from Wasdale and offers everything from slabs of cake to champagne teas.

GETTING THERE From the A595 at Holmrook, follow the minor road through Santon to Nether Wasdale.

MORE INFO golakes.co.uk

OTHER UNDISCOVERED CORNERS
• Rannoch Moor, Scotland (undiscoveredscotland.com)
• Hengwm Valley, Wales (tourism.powys.gov.uk)
• Knoydart Peninsula, Scotland (undiscoveredscotland.com)

22 A Theatrical Treat
MINACK, ENGLAND

Settle in for an evening performance of a play, opera or musical at this breathtaking outdoor theatre, cut into the edge of the Cornish cliffs.

What could be more perfect than a warm summer's evening, some alfresco theatre and views of the sparkling Atlantic stretching out into the distance? The spectacularly located Minack Theatre offers all three in abundance, built into a gully on the beautiful headland of the same name. The theatre represents the work and lifelong passion of one woman, Rowena Cade, whose original idea it was to build the Minack in the 1930s and who continued to oversee and run it until it became a charitable trust in the mid-1970s.

Thanks to the determination of Cade, Minack's unique history is as much a part of a visit as present-day productions. The theatre is open all year round for day visitors, with a cafe and visitor centre that charts the development of the Minack and

Cade's integral role. From May to September there is a varied programme of plays, opera and musicals which change

RIGHT. A performance of The Three Musketeers *at Minack is transformed into a magical experience on a warm night, with the sea lapping gently at the foot of the cliffs.*

each week – and nothing but the heaviest rain and winds tends to stop the performances going ahead.

The Minack is situated at the most distant tip of Cornwall in the small village of Porthcurno, just 10 minutes from Lands End and 20 minutes from the port of Penzance. The beach that lies beneath the theatre is stunning: high cliffs on both sides and a sweeping curve of white sand. Ideal for families – a stream runs down on one side of the beach that is great for kids to paddle in, while teenagers can make the most of the waves with surf or body boards.

A short drive away lies Sennen Cove, which boasts one of Cornwall's most beautiful beaches. Whitesand offers fantastic

surfing, as it catches both the northerly current and southerly winds and Sennen itself has retained the feel of a small fishing village. The South West Coast Path links Porthcurno to Lands End and Sennen, and it's a dramatically beautiful walk with rock stacks and cliffs that sheer down to the sea.

Garden lovers are always well catered for in Cornwall, and there are several stunning gardens to visit around Penzance. Trengwainton (nationaltrust.org) is home to some magnificent walled gardens that grow species of plants not seen anywhere else in Britain, while Trewidden (trewiddengarden.co.uk) dates back to the 19th century and has the biggest collection of camellias in the UK. Penzance itself is well worth a visit, with a lattice of picturesque streets twisting down to the harbour, dotted with cosy pubs and fish restaurants serving up the catch of the day.

But a stay in this area of Cornwall is really all about the coast, whether perched on the stone seats at the Minack, or catching waves at stunning Lamorna or Sennen. The waters are home to plenty of wildlife too, and perhaps the greatest pleasure is relaxing with a cold beer or a cream tea and catching sight of the dolphins and seals that glide past the Minack and the waters around Sennen; a truly magical moment.

INFORMATION

STAY The **Old Success** (01736 871232; staustellbrewery.co.uk) is a cosy 17th century fisherman's inn, with 12 comfortable rooms, in a fantastic position right on the beach at Sennen Cove. Beach lovers should book the **Wearhouse** (porthcurno-apartment.co.uk), a cosy apartment, sleeping up to four, within walking distance of the sands at Porthcurno Bay. **Treen Farm Campsite** (07958 469322; treenfarmcampsite.co.uk) has excellent facilities, including an on-site shop and is within walking distance from two beautiful beaches.

EAT The **Cable Station Inn** (01736 810479; cablestationinn.co.uk) is within walking distance of the Minack and specializes in dishes using locally sourced food. For a memorable evening, **Beach** (01736 871191; thebeachrestaurant.com) – located right by the sea at Sennen – serves up fresh pizza, locally sourced meats and fish along with an all-day children's menu. The **Gurnard's Head** (01736 796928; gurnardshead.co.uk), a short drive from Minack, is one of the best places to eat in the area and has a spectacular location; a daily changing menu of fresh fish and local produce, with stunning views out to sea.

GETTING THERE Turn off the B3315 at the sign to St Levan and follow the road to Porthcurno.

MORE INFO minack.com; visitcornwall.com

OTHER GREAT ALFRESCO THEATRES
• Regent's Park Open Air Theatre, London (openairtheatre.org)
• Oxford Shakespeare Company (oxfordshakespearecompany.co.uk)
• Ludlow Festival (ludlowfestival.co.uk)

23 Go Up in a Balloon
BRISTOL, ENGLAND

Join the biggest Balloon Fiesta in Europe when up to 150 huge, colourful balloons take to the skies above the city of Bristol in a spectacular show.

There is something quite unique about the sight of a hot-air balloon gliding silently across the sky. In an age when air travel has become more of an irritation than something to be marvelled at, it's ironic that old-fashioned ways of taking flight – from gliding to hot-air ballooning – have never been more popular. Bristol's annual International Balloon Fiesta gets bigger and more spectacular every year, and is now the largest event of its kind in Europe, with hundreds of balloons taking to the skies (weather permitting).

The Fiesta takes place over four days and is free to attend, with around half a million people coming to see the mass ascents (numbering up to 150 balloons), which take place at 6 a.m. and 6 p.m. each day. Alongside

BELOW: A feast of colour and action.

the ascents there is all-day entertainment at the central arena, and the famous 'Bristol Nightglow' each evening, when 30 or more balloons glow in time to music. For those who want to experience a balloon flight, many of the companies taking part offer pre-bookable flights in their balloons.

The summer is a great time to visit Bristol, as there is a huge amount to see and do that is outdoors. Start off with a walking tour along the Brunel Mile; a free audio tour can be downloaded to MP3 players (visitbristol.co.uk) that gives an insight into the city and the role of its most famous son, Isambard Kingdom Brunel. The walk finishes at the SS *Great Britain*, the world's first ocean liner, impressively restored to give an idea of how life would have been for Victorian travellers. Equally worth seeing is the Clifton Suspension Bridge, designed by Brunel and completed after his death, and which remains the iconic symbol of Bristol.

But there is more to the city than its past. Bristol is a city with several different quarters, and the best way to discover them is simply to wander. In the Old City, St Nicholas Market is great for browsing, with stalls selling books, clothing and food – although the best culinary supplies are to be found on Wednesdays, when the farmers' market takes place. Nearby, the Arts Quarter has undergone significant regeneration, and is home to some excellent pubs and quirky stores. A little further afield, Clifton Village is a charming area, with leafy streets home to individual boutiques, galleries and cafes.

Bristol is a city with a very contemporary feel, and a strong cultural and artistic vibe. Visit the Arnolfini (arnolfini.org), where the programme of dance, cinema, exhibitions and talks makes it one of the leading centres for the contemporary arts in Europe. Younger visitors will love At Bristol (at-bristol.org.uk), an interactive science centre and planetarium that helps kids make sense of science through hands-on activities. But on a sunny day there are few things more pleasant than strolling along Bristol's regenerated harbour area, where restaurants and cafes spill out onto terraces by the riverside, perfect for a long, lazy lunch.

BELOW: St Nicholas Market. OPPOSITE: Clifton Suspension Bridge at night.

INFORMATION

STAY Mix summer in the city with some countryside charms, by staying at **Brook Lodge Farm** (01934 862311; brooklodgefarm.com), which has tent and caravan pitches and excellent facilities. To be right in the heart of things, stay at the boutique **Brooks Guesthouse** (0117 930 0066; brooksguesthousebristol.com) next to St Nicholas Market, which has stylish rooms and a cute courtyard garden. If it's a romantic weekend away, book one of the spectacular loft suites at the **Hotel du Vin** (0845 365 4438; hotelduvin.com), housed in cleverly converted 18th-century warehouses.

EAT Foodies should head to **Bordeaux Quay** (0117 906 5559; bordeaux-quay.co.uk), which combines restaurant, wine bar, deli, bakery and cookery school in a stunning location right on the harbour. The **Clifton Kitchen** (0117 946 7870; cliftonkitchen.com) has a rich history, located on the site of Keith Floyd's first restaurant. Food is Modern British, with a great line in weekend brunches. Hearty, locally sourced dishes, yummy pies and good veggie options are on the menu at the **Windmill** (0117 963 5440; barwarsltd.com), along with an excellent range of beers and ciders.

MORE INFO
bristolballoonfiesta.co.uk

GETTING THERE From the M4 follow the M32 to Bristol.

OTHER BALLOON FESTIVALS
• Northampton Balloon Festival (thenorthamptonballoonfestival. co.uk)
• Llangollen Balloon Festival (llangollen.org.uk)
• Tiverton Balloon Festival (tivertonballoonfestival.co.uk)

24 Ride the Jack Mytton Way
SHROPSHIRE, ENGLAND

Shropshire is one of England's most tranquil and beautiful counties, and a weekend on horseback is the perfect way to discover its charms.

Turn off any of the main roads that run through Shropshire and you're instantly transported back in time by about 30 years. This rural county is criss-crossed by country lanes that are usually free of signposts, and it's very easy to get lost among the sleepy villages and rural farms. But then rural Shropshire is not really the place for a car; this is riding country, where you are more likely to see horses than cars on the roads, and countless bridleways run across the hills.

One of the best horse-riding trails in Shropshire is the Jack Mytton Way, a route that runs for almost 160km (100 miles), named after a local bad boy 'Mad Jack' Mytton. Jack boozed, gambled and partied his way through a fortune in the early 19th century, and it's somewhat ironic that his name graces a route that is all about peace and tranquillity.

The trail starts in Cleobury Mortimer and takes in the picturesque villages of Church Stretton and Clun, as well as the larger town of Bridgnorth and the Olympic village of Much Wenlock. Local stables can arrange day, overnight or even week-long rides – Country Treks (horsetreks.co.uk) offer rides for all levels of experience. There is also a 'southern loop' part of the trail, which can be done in two to three days, and offers the chance to explore some of the least-visited parts of Shropshire.

Whether on horseback or in a car, there is much to see and do in this part of the world. The village of Much Wenlock is famous as the birthplace of the modern Olympic Games – first held in 1850 and still an annual event. To the south, Clun (clun.org.uk) is one of England's most picturesque villages, lying in a wooded valley, and built around a 14th-century

OPPOSITE ABOVE LEFT: Elizabethan houses in Much Wenlock. ABOVE RIGHT: Iron Bridge. BELOW: A peaceful bridleway on a sunny summer's day – bliss!

INFORMATION

STAY Shropshire is rural England at its most idyllic, and there is some great farm-stay accommodation. **Dinney Farm** (01746 861070; thedinney.co.uk), near to Bridgnorth, offers B&B and self-catering in luxurious cottages with beautiful views over the Severn Valley. The **Hundred House Hotel** (01952 580240; hundredhouse.co.uk), close to Ironbridge, is a fabulously quirky hotel with luxury rooms and award-winning food. Caravanners and campers are well catered for at **Sytche** (01952 727491; sytchecaravanandcamping.co.uk), a lovely rural site just a short walk from Much Wenlock.

EAT For a hit of the Med in the heart of England, drop into Bridgnorth's **Casa Ruiz** (01746 218084; casaruiz.co.uk), which offers fantastic tapas with lots of good veggie options. Home-made cooking of the most comforting sort is on offer at the **Copper Kettle** (01952 728419) in Much Wenlock: great pies, cakes and muffins. Serious foodies should book in for dinner at the 16th-century **Fox Inn** (01952 727292; the-fox-inn.co.uk) in Much Wenlock, where proprietor and ex-Savoy chef John Davison does wonderful things with local Shropshire produce.

MORE INFO
shropshire.gov.uk

GETTING THERE Bridgnorth and Much Wenlock are accessed from junctions 4–6 of the M54.

OTHER GREAT RIDING TRAILS
• The Coleridge Way, Somerset (coleridgeway.co.uk)
• The Newtondale Horse Trail, Yorkshire (northyorkmoors.org.uk)
• The Brecon Beacons, Wales (horseridingbreconbeacons.com)

packhorse bridge, which still stands today. The remains of Norman Clun Castle and the Jacobean almshouses are also both worth visiting.

Although Shropshire is now mostly an agricultural county, in the 19th century it was the birthplace of the Industrial Revolution. The world's first cast-iron bridge was built to cross the river Severn in 1779 and still stands today, along with some of the furnaces, factories and workshops that produced ceramics, tiles, coal and iron. The area is a UNESCO World Heritage Site and has been developed into an impressive visitor attraction (ironbridge.org.uk) with

10 museums, along with Blists Hill – a recreated Victorian high street where visitors can stroll, shop and eat, and chat to shopkeepers who are in Victorian character. The area is also home to an excellent microbrewery (ironbridgebrewery.co.uk) that offers tastings and a good choice of beers to take away.

These days it's hard to imagine Shropshire as an industrial centre; the rolling hills are peaceful and the air is crisp and fresh. Whether an experienced horse rider or a complete novice, it's the perfect place to discover the history and beauty of the great British countryside.

25 A Day at the Races
CHESTER, ENGLAND

Dust off your best summer hat and head to one of England's most unique and walkable cities for a flutter on the horses and a spree in the shops.

A day at the races is a particularly British pleasure; think Audrey Hepburn in *My Fair Lady*, the ostentatious headgear at Ascot Ladies Day – even the Queen Mother was allegedly an avid reader of the *Racing Post*. Racing festivals are a great excuse to glam up and glug a glass or three of champagne, and since the Chester Festival takes place in May there's a chance of some glorious warm sunshine too.

BELOW: Experience the roar of the crowd as the horses enter the home straight and head for the winning post – perhaps with a pound or two riding on the outcome.

The May Festival opens the racing season at Chester (chester-races.co.uk), and on the second day the glam factor is upped considerably – the Boodles Ladies Day is when the serious dressing up takes place. The joy of a day at the races is that it doesn't have to cost a fortune, with open tickets (which just give access to the racecourse rather than to a particular stand) available for under a tenner. It's also possible to walk to the racecourse from the centre of town, making it perfect as part of a weekend city break.

Chester is one of the UK's most elegant cities, steeped in Roman history and famous for the 'Rows': covered walkways at first-floor level which lead to entrances to shops. Beneath them, at street level, lies another row of shops and the upper galleries are believed to date back to medieval times, when they may have been built on the rubble of Roman buildings. The Rows are found in the four main city streets in Chester and are totally unique; there is nothing similar anywhere in the world. The city is also famous for the imposing walls that encircle it – the most complete in the country, with the north and east sections following the old line of the Roman walls.

The city benefits from being built around the river Dee, and if the weather is warm getting out on the water can be a lovely way to spend an afternoon. ChesterBoat (chesterboat.co.uk) runs cruises of varying lengths along the river,

BELOW: *The Queen's Park Suspension Bridge for pedestrians spans the river Dee.* INSET OPPOSITE: *Chester is famous for its half-timbered buildings.*

INFORMATION

STAY If money is no object, the best address in town is the **Chester Grosvenor** (01244 324024; chestergrosvenor.com), which offers gloriously swanky rooms, a small but luxurious spa and two restaurants; one with a Michelin star. For something smaller, but still stylish, boutique **Dragonfly** (01244 346740; hoteldragonfly.com) offers sleek bedrooms in a Grade II listed Georgian town house, in the heart of the city. If you fancy self-catering, **Commonhall Apartments** (07813 764301; commonhallapartments.com) are located in a restored 400-year-old building in the centre of town, with views along the famous Rows.

EAT The **Pied Bull** (01244 325829; piedbull.co.uk) is reputedly the oldest pub in Chester, dating back to the mid-12th century, and serving up luscious steaks and fresh fish dishes that change daily. The **Blue Moon Cafe** (01244 322481; bluemooncafe.eu) is a local favourite, a 1950s-themed eatery on the banks of the river Dee that does a great line in hearty breakfasts. Combine an afternoon's racing with an indulgent lunch or supper at **1539** (01244 304611; restaurant1539.co.uk), a spectacular dining room with stunning views overlooking the racecourse.

GETTING THERE Chester Racecourse is located in the heart of the city, on New Crane Street (A548).

MORE INFO visitchester.com

OTHER RACECOURSES
• Goodwood, Sussex (goodwood.co.uk)
• Aintree, Merseyside (aintree.co.uk)
• Cheltenham, Gloucestershire (cheltenham.co.uk)

---

some of which take in the beautiful Eaton Estate, home of the Duke and Duchess of Westminster. To explore further, Chester Day Boat Hire (chesterdayboathire.co.uk) offer canal boats for up to eight people, which can be rented for a day's exploration of the tranquil Chester Canal.

There's plenty to do if you've got the kids in tow. Chester Zoo (chesterzoo.org) is a great day out, with over 7,000 animals in the 44-ha (110-acre) park. The Grosvenor Park Miniature Railway (gpmr.co.uk) is another good option for younger kids, with steam- and diesel-hauled trains chugging along a quarter-of-a-mile circuit around the lake in Grosvenor Park. The city also has fabulous shopping potential; alongside all the familiar stores there are lesser-known corners of town, such as Rufus Court (rufuscourt.co.uk), that are home to individual boutiques and businesses. The beauty of Chester is that everything – from the Roman walls to the racecourse itself – is all within strolling distance, making it a relaxing city-break destination – a rare find indeed.

26 Set Sail on the Solent
THE HAMBLE, ENGLAND

Spend a weekend learning to sail on the calm waters between the Hampshire coast and the Isle of Wight, or ambling in the country parks of the Hamble Valley.

For most travellers, the strip of coast around Southampton and Portsmouth is only visited as a point of departure for somewhere else: to catch the ferries that run to northern France or the Isle of Wight, or the mammoth cruise ships that leave Southampton's port for exotic destinations around the world. Few, besides locals and sailors, are aware that between the two cities lies the Hamble Valley – a lush, unspoiled river valley that is rich in wildlife and family attractions and one of the best places in the country to learn to sail.

The Hamble flows into the Solent – the stretch of water between the south coast and the Isle of Wight – and the double tides, deep water and easy access to the Solent make it a fantastic place to sail. In the summer months the water is busy with events and regattas, and even those who choose to stay on dry land feel part of the sailing community. There are three marinas and four sailing clubs along the Hamble, with companies catering for every level of sailor, from absolute beginner to experienced yachtsman.

The Hamble is home to the Royal Yachting Association (rya.org.uk), which runs learn-to-sail courses that last from two days up to a full week, with a choice of craft including dinghies, small keelboats and multihulls. Speed freaks can opt for a day's powerboating, and there are courses tailored for children. There are also plenty of companies such as Blue Funnel (02380 223278; bluefunnel.co.uk) that offer cruises around the area where there's nothing to do but simply sit back and enjoy the view. Weekend 'learn-to-sail' courses generally include a brief information session on the basic techniques of sailing and a day spent pottering up and down the Hamble before venturing out in the wider waters of the Solent.

OPPOSITE: The Sigma 33 class provides some of the tightest racing of the Cowes Week regatta.

Back on dry land, there are some beautiful country parks in the Hamble Valley that are ideal for a summer picnic. Visit the Itchen Valley Country Park, which has waymarked trails running through the 178ha (440 acres) of grounds, or the Royal Victoria Country Park, which combines lush woods with open parkland, and spectacular views of the surrounding countryside from the top of the Chapel Tower. Manor Farm Country Park is ideal if you've younger children in tow; they'll love the working Victorian farm where they can meet and pet the animals and learn about traditional farming.

The Hamble Valley is also known as the Strawberry Coast – named after the strawberry fields around Botley, Hedge End and Titchfield that once produced around

ABOVE: Sunset on the Solent – what could be more beautiful or more tranquil?
OPPOSITE: Etchells class sloops race during Cowes Week.

20,000 strawberries a season. There is even a waymarked 'Strawberry Trail', a 24-km (15-mile) circular trail that begins and ends in Botley, with plenty of places to pause en route for a spot of afternoon tea. Blue skies, lush countryside and a bowl of strawberries and cream; what could possibly be more British?

INFORMATION

STAY Idyllically situated overlooking the river Hamble, **Compass Point** (07850 775020; compasspointhamble.co.uk) is a pretty 18th-century Georgian house with four comfortable bedrooms. Camping and caravanning of every type are catered for at the **Riverside Holidays** site (02380 453220; shambaholidays.co.uk/riverside-holidays/) with touring facilities alongside static vans and luxury lodges. If you want to mix sailing with some indulgent spa treatments, book the **Solent Hotel & Spa** (01489 880000; solenthotel.com) near Fareham, which has a beautiful pool, therapeutic saunas and a wide range of treatments.

EAT Check out the catch of the day at the **Jolly Farmer** (01489 572500; thejollyfarmer.uk.com), a traditional pub in Warsash that serves up hearty grills and pies alongside locally caught fish. For a classy lunch, the **River Rat Cellar & Kitchen** (02380 457801; riverrathamble.co.uk) in Hamble offers beautifully presented dishes such as pork loin with apricot puree and sea bass with rocket. Afternoon tea doesn't come much better than at **Lillys** (01329 830305; lillyswickham.com) in Wickham, where doorstep sandwiches and home-made cakes are accompanied by pots of tea, coffee or even a glass of champagne.

MORE INFO hamblevalley.com

GETTING THERE Leave the M27 at junction 8 and follow the B3397 to Hamble.

OTHER GREAT LEARN-TO-SAIL LOCATIONS
• The Norfolk Broads (norfolksailingschool.co.uk)
• The Firth of Clyde (westcoastsailing.co.uk)
• The Lleyn Peninsula (abersochsailingschool.com)

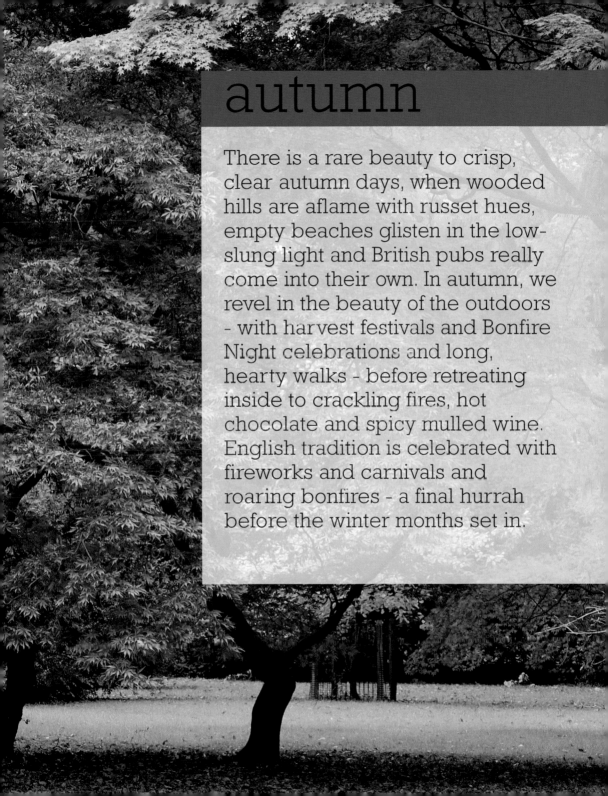

autumn

There is a rare beauty to crisp, clear autumn days, when wooded hills are aflame with russet hues, empty beaches glisten in the low-slung light and British pubs really come into their own. In autumn, we revel in the beauty of the outdoors - with harvest festivals and Bonfire Night celebrations and long, hearty walks - before retreating inside to crackling fires, hot chocolate and spicy mulled wine. English tradition is celebrated with fireworks and carnivals and roaring bonfires - a final hurrah before the winter months set in.

27 A Festival of Food
ABERGAVENNY, WALES

Forget the diet and let your taste buds be tempted by local delicacies and visiting chefs at one of the most popular food festivals in the country

Most visitors to South Wales cross the Severn Bridge and keep their foot firmly on the accelerator – heading for the stunning beaches of the Pembrokeshire coast or the beautiful, lush valleys of Mid Wales. Hurtling straight past Abergavenny means that most also miss the dramatic Brecon Beacons National Park – one of the least visited parks in the country. This overlooked corner of Wales offers an unbeatable combination of outdoor pursuits, foodie treats and a burgeoning art scene – perfect for an autumn weekend.

Food is integral to a stay in Abergavenny at any time – the agricultural economy that has always sustained the area has developed into an impressive breed of gastro-tourism in recent years. The town still has a thriving market, packed with stalls selling cheeses, cured meats, artisan breads and fruit and vegetables pulled from the ground that day – and the town itself has an agreeable bustle. But it is during the annual food festival

(abergavennyfoodfestival.com) that the town becomes flooded with chefs and food writers, local producers and foodie buffs.

The Food Festival was founded in 1999 by two local farmers who saw it as a way of doing something positive after the BSE crisis. It was one of the first food festivals in the country and draws top culinary names each year, including Antonio Carluccio, Anthony Bourdain and Hugh Fearnley-Whittingstall, with a programme of events including talks and tastings, debates and masterclasses. There are also children's events, including interactive workshops.

Aber itself is the 'gateway' to the Beacons (breconbeacons.org) – and the imposing Black Mountains loom in the distance. This is fantastic walking country and there are some memorable walks to the peaks of both the Sugar Loaf and the Skirrid. But you don't have to trek miles; from the Brecon Beacons Visitor Centre a short walk up the moorland ridge of Mynydd Illtyd

RIGHT: *Shoppers select herbs from a Food Festival market stall.* BELOW: *Sugarloaf Mountain, to the north-west of Abergavenny, framed by vivid autumn colour. Its 596m (1,955ft) summit rewards walkers with sweeping panoramic views.*

gives breathtaking views across four counties. The Beacons are also rich in history, with Iron Age hill forts such as Garn Goch, Neolithic standing stones and Norman castles – the most dramatic of which is Carreg Cennen. The Visitor Centre has a wide range of maps, walking itineraries and ideas for different ways to discover this wild and unspoiled area of Wales.

The Visitor Centre is just a short drive from the charming town of Brecon, and pairing a walk in the Beacons with lunch and a stroll around Brecon makes a great day out from Aber. There is a strong arts and crafts community, and the town's Arts Trail (artbeatbrecon.co.uk) is an excellent guide to the galleries and studios that dot the town's streets. Glassmakers, artists and interior designers are all on the map, and most are delighted to talk about their work with visitors.

But perhaps the most charming place to visit near Abergavenny is Usk Castle (uskcastle.com), a ruined Norman castle that overlooks the village of Usk. Privately owned, it is charmingly quirky with a pair of geese as the castle guards and is an apt metaphor for this entire slice of border country: tucked away, little known and utterly delightful.

INFORMATION

STAY Situated just outside Aber, **Clare Cottage** (breconcottages.com) is a delightful 100-year-old bolt-hole with gorgeous views of the Sugarloaf Mountain. Stay at the heart of the action at the **Angel** (01873 857121; angelhotelabergavenny.co.uk), with luxurious, reasonably priced rooms and a great restaurant. Catch the last of the summer by taking the caravan or tent, and stay at the **Blossom Touring Caravan Park** (01873 850444; blossompark.co.uk), which has super-sized pitches and excellent facilities.

EAT The **Walnut Tree Inn** (01873 852797; thewalnuttreeinn.com), 3.2 kilometres (2 miles) outside Aber, is a must-visit for foodies. The menu changes almost daily according to the local produce available. The **Hardwick** (01873 854220; thehardwick.co.uk) is another excellent gastropub, with a diverse menu ranging from ham, egg and chips to diver-caught scallops with polenta chips. Famed as the place for the moistest, most luscious cakes in the area, **For the Love of Cakes** (23 Frogmore Street) is the perfect place for a restorative cupcake after strolling around the busy market.

GETTING THERE Follow the A40 from the southern end of the M5, or take the A449 from the M4 and join the A40 at Raglan.

MORE INFO
visitabergavenny.co.uk

OTHER FOOD FESTIVALS
• Ludlow Marches Food and Drink Festival, Shropshire (foodfestival.co.uk)
• Eat! NewcastleGateshead Food Festival (eatnewcastlegateshead.com)
• Scottish Food Fortnight (scottishfoodanddrinkfortnight .co.uk)

28 Marvel at the Maples
WESTONBIRT, ENGLAND

The National Arboretum in Gloucestershire explodes with colour in the autumn months, as the acer groves and maple glades fire up in sherbet shades of pink, orange and yellow.

There are few greater pleasures in life than an autumn walk: a crisp blue sky, the ground hard under foot, the trees resplendent in shades of flame and sherbet. In October and November, our woods turn butter and saffron, warm auburn and mulberry-red. But

BELOW: Westonbirt ablaze with colour.

for truly blazing colours – the hot raspberry and tangerine of Japanese acers and the lemon-yellow of maples – there is no better place to visit than the National Arboretum at Westonbirt, one of the most spectacular collections of trees in the world.

Tucked away in the Gloucestershire countryside, Westonbirt was a privately owned estate until it was handed over to the Forestry Commission in the 1950s. Before that, it was owned by the wealthy Holford family for over 200 years, and when their involvement with the American Gold Rush increased their fortunes in the 19th century, the arboretum gradually took shape. Once the Forestry Commission took over, the tree collection was added to and the estate was landscaped to make it more visitor-friendly. Westonbirt today is home to an awe-inspiring number of trees: from imposing oaks and statuesque pines to blossom-clad cherry trees.

A trip to Westonbirt can be easily tied in to a stay in the elegant town of Bath, around 27km (17 miles) away. Autumn is an excellent time to visit, with the hills around the city glowing in their autumn colours and the city's streets free of the hordes of

OPPOSITE LEFT: Few hot pools have a more spectacular setting than that of the Thermae Bath Spa. RIGHT: Castle Combe.

INFORMATION

STAY If you've got the kids in tow, the **Priory Inn** (01666 502251; theprioryinn.co.uk) in Tetbury is a great option – the staff are very family-friendly, there are good kids' facilities and children under 12 stay free if sharing a room with parents. Keep it natural with a stay under canvas at **Burton Hill** campsite (01666 826880; burtonhill.co.uk) near Malmesbury, a beautiful riverside site. For an indulgent weekend based in Bath, book the **Queensberry** (01225 447928; thequeensberry.co.uk), a stylish hotel with a fabulous restaurant, the Olive Tree.

EAT Tetbury is a rich source of eating options; try the **Chef's Table** (thechefstable.co.uk) – part deli, part fishmonger, part bistro – and the brainchild of Michael Bedford, protégé of Raymond Blanc. For a traditional Cotswolds lunch, try the **Snooty Fox** (01666 502436; snooty-fox.co.uk), which combines a cosy pub feel with hotel accommodation. You can't visit Bath without dropping into **Sally Lunns** cafe (01225 461364; sallylunns.co.uk), home of the original Bath bun and the oldest house in the city.

GETTING THERE Exit the M4 at Junction 18. Take the A46 towards Stroud, and turn right at the A433 towards Cirencester. After 5km (3 miles) the Arboretum is on the left.

MORE INFO forestry.gov.uk/westonbirt

OTHER GREAT PLACES FOR AUTUMN COLOURS
• The National Forest, Midlands (nationalforest.org)
• Exbury Gardens, Hampshire (exbury.co.uk)
• The Outwoods, Leicestershire (charnwood.gov.uk)

summer tourists and not yet overrun by Christmas shoppers. Any visit to Bath should include a stop at the Thermae Bath Spa (thermaebathspa.com), which combines 21st-century spa treatments with the city's thermal waters, which have been used for health and recreation purposes since Roman times.

For somewhere smaller and less hectic, the picturesque village of Castle Combe (castle-combe.com) makes a great place for lunch and a gentle stroll. Steeped in history, the village began life as a British hill fort that was occupied by the Romans, and then the Normans who built the fort into a castle. By the Middle Ages the village had become an important centre for the wool industry and many of the houses from this period still line the quiet streets. Pop into the White Hart for a warming pint or spot of lunch, before visiting the small but informative village museum and taking a quiet moment in the 15th-century church.

There is so much to do in this area that a weekend is far too short: the pretty Cotswold village of Tetbury is just 10 minutes from Westonbirt, Stonehenge is a short drive away and the famous Wiltshire White Horse – carved into the chalky hills – makes the perfect focus for a long country walk. There are beautiful stately homes to visit too, such as Stourhead (nationaltrust.org) and Longleat (longleat.co.uk). But no sight is as spectacular as the blazing colours at Westonbirt – nature at its most wonderfully vibrant, making a truly memorable weekend.

29 Ride the Waves
WATERGATE BAY, ENGLAND

Beg, borrow or steal a wetsuit, and learn to surf or bodyboard (or just paddle around) in the waters off one of Cornwall's most spectacular beaches.

There's something not very English about Cornwall's Atlantic coastline. It's too dramatic: swooping cliffs that hunker down against swathes of buttery sand, glistening rock pools battered by white-topped rollers that rear up and hurl themselves towards land with a fury built up all the way across from the eastern seaboard of the US. There's a wildness to it, and an egalitarianism; Cornwall's beaches are a playground for everyone – from those staying in beachfront campsites to those ensconced in five-star glamour in the new breed of chic hotels.

BELOW: Non-surfing visitors to Watergate Bay can enjoy a peaceful walk along its sands, or munch hot chips at the beachfront cafe.

Early autumn is the best time to hit the Cornish coast if you're in search of waves, and Watergate Bay is one of the best options, whether you're kitesurfing, bodyboarding, or straightforward stand-up-and-fall-over surfing. The summer crowds will have dissipated slightly and this glorious 3-km (2-mile) stretch of beach plays host to long, slow rollers that are perfect for beginner bodyboarders or practised surfers. Lifeguards keep a constant watch, and along with the hire shop and surf school, there is the Watergate Bay Extreme Academy, where you can learn to kitesurf, power-kite or, um, wave-ski (whatever that may be).

Watergate Bay has been saved from overdevelopment because there is still just one small road that leads down to the beach. It's famous now as the first outpost of Jamie Oliver's 19 restaurants, but even that celebrity endorsement hasn't ruined its drama and beauty. The beachfront (non-Jamie) cafe does hot chocolates and bacon sandwiches and there are showers and toilets should you need them.

If you're lucky enough to stay in Watergate Bay itself, you may not wish to go anywhere else for the weekend – but there is plenty to experience nearby. One trip into Newquay may well be enough; excellent for purchases of hot pasties and hoodies – ideal

INFORMATION

STAY You can't get closer to the action than staying at the **Watergate Bay Hotel** (01637 860543; watergatebay.co.uk), right on the beach, with chic rooms and a very social atmosphere. **Morland House** (01637 860802; stmawganbandb.co.uk) is a stylish B&B between Watergate and Mawgan Porth, run on eco-principles and with a beautiful sunroom. **Watergate Bay Touring Park** (01637 860387; watergatebaytouringpark. co.uk) is ideal for young families, with camping and caravanning pitches.

EAT If you want to eat at **Fifteen Cornwall** (01637 861000; fifteencornwall.co.uk) be sure to book ahead; worth it for reliably rustic Jamie recipes and great views of the beach. The **Falcon Inn** (01637 860255; thefalconinn-stmawgan.co.uk), at nearby St Mawgan, serves up hearty portions of good food in a beautiful 16th-century building, while tea and cake don't come in more spectacular surroundings than the National Trust tea shop at **Carnewas** (nationaltrust.org.uk), which has spectacular views across Bedruthan Beach and the famous Bedruthan Steps.

GETTING THERE From Newquay, take the B3276 north, through Porth, for about 6km (4 miles). Newquay airport, which has flights to several regional airports, is five minutes' drive from Watergate Bay.

MORE INFO
visitcornwall.com/site/things-to-do/beaches

OTHER GREAT SURFING BEACHES
• Croyde Bay, Devon (northdevon.com)
• Llangennith, Gower (visitswanseabay.com)
• Thurso East, Highland (caithness.org)

ABOVE: A kitesurfer experiences the challenge of mastering wave and wind power for a thrilling ride over the rollers of Watergate Bay.

for keeping warm on a windy beach – but unless you feel the need for a cut-price pub crawl, it's probably not necessary to stick more than one hour on the pay-and-display meter. Instead leave the car at the beach and set out on foot; Watergate Bay lies on the South West Coast Path, with Mawgan Porth and Bedruthan Steps to the north, and Newquay and Constantine to the south.

If you have the kids in tow, the Screech Owl Sanctuary (screechowlsanctuary.co.uk) offers a pleasant afternoon, particularly since the introduction of meerkat

residences in 2010. The Bluereef Aquarium in Newquay (bluereefaquarium.co.uk/newquay.htm) is a good bet if the rain comes in, while golf lovers can swap their board for a birdie at the Merlin Golf Club (merlingolfcourse.co.uk) at Mawgan Porth.

But a weekend in Watergate Bay is really all about, well, getting in the water. If you're a novice, be prepared to lose your breath, your balance and your dignity (no one over the age of 21, or bigger than a size eight looks good in a wetsuit). Oh, and to become addicted. Because once you actually catch a wave and feel yourself hurtling towards the shore, you'll understand what it's all about. Glorious fun for all ages.

30 Read All About It
SEDBERGH, ENGLAND

Enjoy fossicking for rare and second-hand books in England's only book town, tucked away in a tranquil corner of the magnificent Dales.

The fate of the small, unassuming town of Sedbergh was changed forever in 2003, after foot-and-mouth disease had taken its toll on the number of visitors to the region. The Sedbergh Book Town company was created with the aim of developing a community of businesses involved in selling, writing and publishing books. Over the next few years, a number of independent booksellers were lured to set up shop in the town. Nine years later it remains England's only official book town, alongside Hay-on-Wye in Wales and Wigtown in Scotland.

The high point for book lovers is the literary festival in September, where local writers such as Booker Prize nominee Sarah Hall and children's author John Rice hold workshops and talks, but literary matters dominate this sleepy Dales town throughout the year. The streets are dotted with second-hand bookshops and dealers, many offering rare and out-of-print titles. Dip into Sleepy Elephant (41 Main Street) for rare books on crafts and interiors, or Henry Wilson (61 Main St), which specializes in transport books. Westwood Books on Long Lane and Bertrams on Back Lane both have impressive collections of second-hand and antiquarian books.

In amongst the bookshops, lie traditional family businesses – bakers, butchers and hardware shops. It's worth popping into Fairfield Mill (fairfieldmill.org), a converted woollen mill a mile or so out of town, where over 30 local artists produce and sell their work, alongside exhibitions of local traditional crafts. Sedbergh is far, far from Starbucks territory and all the better for it – an unassuming rural town, tucked away at the westernmost corner of the Yorkshire Dales, but actually in Cumbria.

Besides the books, the other reason for a visit to Sedbergh is to explore the beautiful countryside that surrounds the

OPPOSITE: The Dales: tranquil and unspoiled.

INFORMATION

STAY Recently refurbished, the **Bull Hotel** (01539 620264; bullhotelsedbergh.co.uk) is a cosy 17th-century coaching inn in the heart of town, with comfortably furnished rooms, a friendly, welcoming bar and a more formal restaurant. Cosy up in **Saddlers Cottage** (01539 621389; sedbergh cottages.co.uk), a traditional stone-built house sleeping four, with luxury touches such as home cinema, fluffy towels and a stylish kitchen. To really experience the rural life of the Dales, pitch your tent at **Holme Open Farm** (01539 620654; holmeopenfarm.co.uk) – the farm has an on-site cafe and gift shop, and children can help feed the animals.

EAT The award-winning **Sedbergh Cafe** (01539 621389; thesedberghcafe.com) is a traditional tea room specializing in wedges of indulgent home-made cake. If you're after hearty pub grub, it doesn't come better than at the **Dalesman** (01539 621183; thedalesman.co.uk), where the seasonal menu always includes local produce. If you're heading towards Kendal, the **Punch Bowl Inn** (01539 568237; the-punchbowl.co.uk) is a former winner of the Michelin Guide's pub of the year, offering locally sourced meats and good veggie options.

GETTING THERE Leave the M6 at junction 37 and head east on the A684 towards Sedbergh.

MORE INFO sedbergh.org.uk

OTHER BOOK TOWNS
• Hay-on-Wye, Wales (hay-on-wye.co.uk)
• Wigtown, Scotland (wigtown-booktown.co.uk)

town. The Howgill Fells – made famous by Britain's patron saint of walking, Alfred Wainwright – loom above the town and offer some fantastic walking and hiking trails, rising to around 610m (2,000ft). One of the easiest walks is from the town up to the top of Winder Fell; a climb of around 460m (1,500ft) that offers stunning views across the Lake District hills and the Lune Valley, which stretches down to Morecambe Bay.

It's also great horse-riding territory; the Pennine Bridleway and the Eden Valley Loops offer miles of open fell bridleways and ancient packhorse routes. Stonetrail Riding Centre (01539 623444; stonetrailholidays.

com) in nearby Kirkby Lonsdale can offer rides from one hour to all day. Golfers can potter around the greens of the Sedbergh Golf Club (sedberghgolfclub.co.uk), and the cosy stone-built clubhouse is the perfect spot for a post-round pint.

Further afield the bustling market town of Kendal is well worth a visit, and just a few miles further on lies Windermere, most beautiful of all the Cumbrian lakes. No matter where you visit in this rural corner of the UK, you're guaranteed a truly relaxing break.

31 Splurge on Seafood
LOCH FYNE, SCOTLAND

Gaze at loch or ocean views as you indulge in shellfish platters heaped with crab, lobster, oysters and prawns in the seafood mecca of Scotland's West Coast.

There are few restaurant dishes more spectacular than a seafood platter: heaps of mussels and prawns, gleaming crab and lobster, fresh oysters glistening on crushed ice and watercress. When it's served up in a spectacular location, on the banks of a sparkling sea loch, perhaps, with wooded hills in the distance and a picturesque fishing village behind, the whole experience can be just about perfect. If it

BELOW: A fishing boat heads into Tarbert, Loch Fyne, which has one of the few natural harbours in Scotland.

sounds too good to be true, such a place does exist: Loch Fyne – one of the most beautiful of all Scotland's lochs and home to some of the best seafood in the country.

Loch Fyne has been famous for its fish for over 200 years, although the major haul of herring has been replaced by salmon, along with scallop, langoustine and lobster, which are fished for on a daily basis by small local fleets. The seas in this area of Scotland are so rich that a Seafood Trail (theseafoodtrail.com) links some of the best places to eat and stay in the area. There are several around Loch Fyne, which stretches north from the Clyde Estuary up to Inverary

BELOW: A tranquil view down the length of Loch Fyne from Inveraray.

and beyond, with the Kintyre peninsula stretching south into the sea.

Villages such as Tarbert, Lochgilphead and Inverary make ideal bases for exploring the surrounding countryside and offer the chance to really experience Scottish village life. The small inlet around which Tarbert has grown up has been used as a place of shelter for boats for over a thousand years, with Robert the Bruce's ship said to have been moored in the harbour in the 14th century. The village has strong links with the Scottish hero; the ruined castle that stands high on a hill behind the village was allegedly commissioned by Bruce himself.

Tarbert is also ideally placed for exploring the islands of Jura, Islay, Gigha and Arran with ferries running from points

INFORMATION

STAY Struan House (01880 820190; struan.biz) is idyllically located on the harbour in the village of Tarbert, and has an excellent seafood restaurant along with cosy rooms above. Live like a laird at the **Stonefield Castle Hotel** (08444 146600; oxfordhotelsandinns.com), which has stunning views across the loch from its 32 luxurious rooms and suites. The **Loch Fyne Hotel & Spa** (0844 950 6282; crerarhotels.com) in Inverary is perfect for a relaxing break, with a state-of-the-art spa and hot tub, which has fabulous views out across the water.

EAT The **Loch Fyne Oyster Bar** (01499 600236; lochfyne.com) in Cairndow is the original – and best – in the Loch Fyne chain. Fish and shellfish are cooked in every way imaginable – all delicious. **Creggans Inn** (01369 860279; creggans-inn.co.uk) in Strachur has been welcoming travellers for centuries, and has a traditional cosy bar along with a more formal dining room. The **Seafood Cabin** (01880 760207) on the Skipness Estate near Tarbert is exactly what it says: a wooden cabin serving up wonderful crab rolls, langoustine and smoked trout and salmon (open until end September).

MORE INFO lochfyne.info

GETTING THERE The A83 links all the villages along the coast of Loch Fyne.

OTHER SEAFOOD SPECIALISTS
• Mersea Island, Essex (mersea-Island.com)
• Whitstable, Kent (seewhitstable.com)
• Helford, Cornwall (visitcornwall.com)

along the Kintyre coast. Head south of the village and the peninsula of Kintyre stretches out to the sea, immortalized in Paul McCartney's song 'Mull of Kintyre'. Largely bypassed by tourism, there is a wonderfully unspoiled air to the landscapes that have seen historic battles between clansmen and Vikings, with castles dating back to the 13th century and a rich variety of wildlife including seals, deer and even the highly elusive otters.

Further north, Inverary is another fishing village steeped in history, with the spectacular Inveraray Castle (inveraray-castle.com) – the ancestral home of the Duke of Argyll – the biggest visitor attraction in the area. On a crisp autumn day the countryside around Inverary is perfect for an afternoon exploring on horseback. Argyll Adventure (argylladventure.com) in Inverary offers rides for all abilities, including gentle hacks along the banks of the loch and up into the Duke of Argyll's estate. And, of course, no visit to this area of Scotland would be complete without a dram or two; pop into the world-famous Loch Fyne Whiskies (lfw.co.uk) in Inverary to pick up a bottle or two.

32 Take the Train
CARLISLE, ENGLAND

Experience one of the great rail journeys in Britain on the Settle to Carlisle railway, via the breathtaking Ribblehead Viaduct with its 24 arches.

Britain was one of the first countries in the world to introduce rail travel, and the Victorian era was known as the golden age, with steam trains journeying across one of the most extensive networks in the world. Although many of the routes have been modernized, some of the more spectacular lines are unchanged, none more dramatic than the Settle to Carlisle railway.

Although steeped in history, the line is still part of the regular railway network, and the 116-km (72-mile) route takes passengers on a journey through the Yorkshire Dales, and over the 24 arches of the spectacular Ribblehead Viaduct before plunging into the long tunnel at Blea Moor. The route then winds through the gentle hills of the Eden Valley before arriving into Carlisle – a journey time of around one hour and three quarters.

The line is a great way to explore the stunning Cumbrian and Yorkshire countryside without having to use the car,

and there are plenty of opportunities for day trips and afternoon walks at stops along the route. The bustling town of Carlisle makes an ideal base for a weekend, and offers plenty to discover – an important centre since Roman times, there are medieval dungeons, chambers and passageways to explore, and a Norman keep, which has panoramic views from the top.

No visit to Carlisle is complete without a trip to Hadrian's Wall (hadrians-wall.org), and there is a regular bus service that runs from the city to all the main Roman sites in the central section of the wall. Carlisle itself is home to Tullie House (tulliehouse.co.uk), which has a mind-boggling 188,000 objects dating from prehistoric times through Roman Cumbria, the Dark Ages and the medieval period.

OPPOSITE: The Dalesman steam train storms up the bank from Morcock Tunnel towards Ais Gill Summit, the highest point on the Settle–Carlisle railway route.

ABOVE: It is well worth planning to spend some time in the busy market town of Carlisle. OPPOSITE: The Ribblehead Viaduct is one of the highlights of the trip.

But it is the train itself that offers the most enjoyable day trips – when the journey is just as much a part of the experience as the destination. Disembark at Ribblehead for the chance to see the viaduct from the ground, rather than travelling on top of it – there is a Visitor Centre in the refurbished station building and a small shop selling teas and snacks. Appleby-in-Westmorland is a delightful town with a number of historic buildings, including some lovely 17th-century almshouses and a Norman castle.

Settle (settle.org.uk) is a good place to disembark, as the town is just a short walk from the beautifully renovated station. Unspoiled and traditional in feel, there are some charming shops around the old market place and the Watershed Mill, 10 minutes' stroll out of town, is well worth a visit. Home to the Dalesmade Craft Centre, Rock and Fossil Shop and an excellent cafe, it's a good way to stretch the legs before the return journey.

The line itself carries on all the way to Leeds, but it is the Settle to Carlisle stretch that is truly spectacular. At times it's hard to know what to marvel at more – the stunning landscapes that surround the train line, or the skill and technique of the engineers who managed to design a railway that could navigate them so smoothly.

INFORMATION

STAY **Willowbeck Lodge** (01228 513607; willowbeck-lodge.com) is the type of B&B that mixes the luxuries of a hotel with the warm informality of a guesthouse. Along with scrumptious breakfasts, a set menu is offered for dinner each evening. Stay out of town at the **Crown Hotel** (01228 561888; crownhotelwetheral.co.uk), in the picturesque village of Wetheral, which has a beautiful pool and conservatory restaurant. For a luxury break, the **Hallmark Hotel** (01228 531951; hallmarkhotels.co.uk/carlisle),

in the heart of the town, has a sleek cocktail bar and fantastic health club.

EAT The **Bijou Restaurant** (01228 818588; bijou-restaurant.co.uk) is a charming, small restaurant in the historic quarter, specializing in local ingredients. Combine a healthy veggie meal, or coffee and cake, with some live music, surrounded by works by local artists at the **Foxes Cafe Lounge** (01228 536439; foxescafelounge.co.uk). For a change from hearty food, pop into **Alexandros** (01228 592227; thegreek.co.uk), for some tasty mezes and smokily grilled meats.

MORE INFO settle-carlisle.co.uk

GETTING THERE Leave the M6 at junction 43 and take the A69 to Carlisle.

OTHER GREAT RAILWAY JOURNEYS
• West Highland Line from Glasgow to Fort William (scotrail.co.uk)
• The Cambrian Coast line, Wales (thecambrianline.co.uk)
• The North York Moors line (nymr.co.uk)

33 Join the Carnival
BRIDGWATER, ENGLAND

Join the party as the Somerset countryside bursts into life with the biggest illuminated procession in Europe, involving spectacular floats built by local people during the year.

Forget the Notting Hill Carnival, head to rural Somerset in late autumn and you will find some of the most spectacular illuminated processions in the world. Alongside the traditional Bonfire Night celebrations, blazing themed carts process through the streets of seven towns in Somerset, on different nights in early November. The picturesque market town of Bridgwater hosts one of the biggest carnivals, with around 150,000 people descending on the town to join in the party.

The illuminated floats can be spectacular; some are up to 30m (100ft) long and 5m (16ft) high, with an astonishing 30,000 light bulbs. Designed and built by carnival clubs around Somerset, many local people work on the carts and raise money throughout the year for their one night of glittering glory. The celebrations date back to 1605, the year of the original Gunpowder Plot, and have particular relevance to this area of Somerset, as the originator of the plot, Robert Parsons,

(not Guy Fawkes as commonly thought) was from the village of Nether Stowey.

Tradition is a major part of these carnivals; those involved are still known as 'masqueraders' and the art of 'squibbing' is still practised, when fireworks, which give off thousands of sparks, are held aloft on long wooden poles. Bridgwater's carnival is still held on a Thursday night, followed by 'Black Friday' (the inappropriate name for a day of celebrations), when the local pubs fill with all those involved in creating the floats.

When the celebrations are over, there is much to discover in this rural corner of Britain. Bridgwater lies equidistant between the Quantock Hills and the beautiful towns of Glastonbury and Wells. The Quantocks (thequantockhills.co.uk) are an Area of Outstanding Natural Beauty and are ideal for exploring on horseback; bridle paths lead up over Lydeard Hill and Staple Plain, and there are also some of the best mountain-bike trails in the West Country.

RIGHT: The spectacular floats are a highlight of the Carnival. *BELOW:* Squibbers in action on Bridgwater high street – 140 squibs are let off simultaneously by carnival club members, culminating in loud bangs as each squib extinquishes.

The name of Glastonbury may be synonymous with the world's most famous music festival, but for the other 51 weeks of the year it remains an attractive town, steeped in history and mysticism. The town is dominated by Glastonbury Tor, which rises up from the Somerset plain, and is surrounded by myths – including the Holy Grail and the Arthurian legends. Twenty-first-century Glastonbury has a distinctly 'new-agey' feel, with a community that has grown up around the myths, and a visit to the town gives an interesting insight into one aspect of British history. No visit to Glastonbury is complete without climbing the Tor, which has a ruined tower at its peak, and gives stunning views across the Somerset countryside.

In autumn the Somerset countryside is so beautiful – morning mists and auburn-tinted woods – that it's perfectly possible to spend a weekend in this area without getting in the car. The countryside is latticed with footpaths – from Bridgwater there are easy strolls to North Petherton and Nether Stowey, or longer walks towards the Quantocks – that offer the chance to experience some of the most unspoiled and tranquil countryside in the whole of Britain.

INFORMATION

STAY Bridgwater lies at the heart of agricultural Somerset, and there is some fabulous farm accommodation in the area. **Hunstile** (01278 662358; hunstileorganicfarm.co.uk) is an organic farm that offers delightful bedrooms in the 14th-century farmhouse, and self-catering options. For a waterside retreat, the **Boat & Anchor** (01278 662473; theboatandanchor.co.uk) has 11 comfortable rooms on the banks of the Bridgwater Canal, and a renowned restaurant. If you can brave the cooler nights, **Currypool Mill** (01278 671135; currypoolmill.co.uk) is a beautiful 6-ha (15-acre) site with camping and caravanning pitches.

EAT Tuck into the best local produce at **Clavelshay Barn** (01278 662629; clavelshaybarn.co.uk), a converted stone barn on a working dairy farm that serves imaginative, beautifully put together dishes. Pair a country walk with a restorative lunch at the **Cottage Inn** (01278 732355; thecottageinnkeenthorne.co.uk), which does an excellent Sunday roast. The **Tea Room at Cannington Walled Gardens** (canningtonwalledgardens.co.uk) is a wonderful spot on a sunny afternoon, with plenty of outdoor seating for a tea-and-cake moment.

MORE INFO
visitsomerset.co.uk

GETTING THERE Leave the M5 at junction 24 and follow the A38 to Bridgwater.

OTHER TRADITIONAL BONFIRE NIGHT CELEBRATIONS
• Tar Barrels, Ottery St Mary, Devon (otterytourism.org.uk)
• Lewes Bonfire Night, Sussex (lewesbonfirecouncil.org.uk)
• Penrhos Beach, Anglesey. (holyheadroundtable.com/events)

34 Watch the Deer Rut
EXMOOR, ENGLAND

Journey deep into rural Devon to watch the dramatic deer rutting – an annual mating ritual between these magnificent animals that is one of nature's greatest spectacles.

There is something almost mythical about the red deer that live among the woods and hills of Exmoor. In many ways, the moors belong to them; they have roamed freely since prehistoric times, surviving due to their protection as Royal Game. There are several thousand red deer on Exmoor – the largest concentration in England – but even so they can be hard to find; deer are notoriously shy creatures, and the best chance of seeing them is at dawn or dusk.

The months of October and November offer the best chances of seeing the deer, not least because this is the mating season when the 'rutting' takes place. The largest stags 'round up' their herds in order to show superiority, and there may be fights between rival stags, characterized by locking horns and loud roars (known as belling or bolving). It is a spectacular sight; the red deer is the largest land mammal in

RIGHT: A red deer stag is an unforgettable sight.

the UK, and some stand up to 115cm (45in) high at the shoulder. The best way to experience a rut is on an organized tour with a guide, and several of the visitor

(exmoor-nationalpark.gov.uk) has a programme of guided walks of all lengths and levels of difficulty.

Exmoor is also home to some of the darkest skies in the country, and the autumn months are the best time to see the constellations. Some of the best spots for stargazing are Holdstone Hill, Webbers Post and Anstey Gate – and Exmoor is the only place in England where you can free camp, meaning that you can find the quietest, darkest corner of the moors, pitch your tent and gaze up at the stars in glorious isolation. By day, one of the most beautiful areas of Exmoor is the Doone Valley, named after the book that made the area famous – *Lorna Doone*. There is an easy walk along the river and the valley is an excellent place to spot the wild Exmoor ponies and deer.

One of the other great joys of a visit to Exmoor is simply pottering around the picturesque villages, stopping for a cream tea and picking up some treats from the village shops that stock local farm produce. Dulverton, on the southernmost edge of the park, is particularly pretty, as is Withypool, overlooking the lush Barle Valley and the heathland of Withypool Common. Somehow, this wild corner of England seems to have been bypassed by the pressures and pace of 21st-century life – and is all the better for it.

centres around Exmoor offer these at certain times.

Although one of the smallest national parks, at just 686 sq. km (265 sq. miles), there are many different ways to experience Exmoor. Spreading south from the north Devon coast, it offers the chance to combine coast and countryside with a stay in the beach towns of Porlock and Minehead, or truly rural escapes in villages such as Exford, right in the heart of the moors. It's a great place for a family break, with dozens of activities to try; Exmoor Adventures (exmooradventures.co.uk) offers everything from mountain biking to coasteering and kayaking, while the National Park Authority

ABOVE LEFT: Dunster Castle, near Minehead, was the home of the Luttrell family for more than 600 years. OPPOSITE: Exmoor ponies.

INFORMATION

STAY Cloud Farm Camping (01598 741278; cloudfarmcamping.com) is an absolute gem, tucked away in the Doone Valley, offering camping and self-catering cottages. **The Royal Oak** (01643 831506; royaloakwithypool.co.uk) in Withypool is a lovely rural bolt-hole, with eight cosy bedrooms above a welcoming, traditional pub. For a real sense of escape, **Three Acres Country House** (01398 323730; threeacrescountryhouse.co.uk) is a luxurious B&B in secluded grounds, surrounded by the lush hills of southern Exmoor.

EAT Twin a visit to Dulverton with lunch at **Woods Bar & Restaurant** (01398 324007; woodsdulverton.co.uk), which has a warming log fire and serves modern British cooking with a French twist. No visit to Exmoor is complete without a cream tea, and the **Buttery** (01598 741106; brendonvalley.co.uk/malmsmead.htm) at Malmsmead in the beautiful Doone Valley offers freshly made scones with lashings of cream. The **Royal Oak Inn** (01643 831506; royaloakwithypool.co.uk) in Withypool serves well-made, traditional pub dishes and luscious puds that come heavy with clotted cream.

MORE INFO exmoor-nationalpark.gov.uk

GETTING THERE The A361 runs along the south of Exmoor; the A39 runs into North Dartmoor.

OTHER PLACES TO SEE DEER
• Arne RSPB, Wareham, Dorset (rspb.org.uk)
• The Scottish Highlands (visithighlands.com)
• Bolderwood Deer Sanctuary, New Forest, Hampshire (thenewforest.co.uk)

35 Explore the Night Sky
KIELDER WATER, ENGLAND

Famous for its dark skies, Northumberland is home to one of the best observatories in England, perfect for non-celebrity star spotting.

Remember lying on your back as a child, staring up at the night sky, marvelling at the sheer number of stars twinkling away across the galaxy? The skies can still inspire the same sense of wonder, but on our overcrowded island, the chance to see a night sky free of light pollution can be surprisingly rare. An autumn weekend in Northumberland offers fantastic star-spotting possibilities, particularly if you include a visit to Kielder Water, the largest man-made lake in Europe and home to the darkest skies in England.

It's not just the unpolluted skies that make Kielder such a great place for budding astronomers; the park is also home to the Kielder Observatory (kielderobservatory.org), a permanent base for working astronomers but also a visitor attraction with star-spotting evenings, talks and lectures taking place throughout the year. The observatory is a stunning piece of architecture and is open during the day for visitors, but the astronomical domes are only open to the public during specific events.

There are plenty of other ways to enjoy Kielder besides the observatory. The 43-km (27-mile) walking route around the lake's coastline now has 20 pieces of outdoor public art along the way. The coastal route is designed for cyclists and horse riders as well as wheelchair users, with plenty of access to the lakeside at its most scenic points. For those in search of more high-octane thrills, Zonks Mountain Tower offers abseiling and rock climbing, while the 150-m (492-ft) zip wire offers a real white-knuckle ride. Low ropes courses, archery and indoor climbing are also on offer, and if it all gets a little exhausting there's the option of recovering on board the Happy Days motor cruiser, which visits some of the most hidden corners of the lake.

Kielder lies at the heart of one of the last great English wildernesses: the

RIGHT: At night, settle in for a memorable session of star gazing and planet spotting at Kielder Observatory. BELOW: In daylight hours Kielder Water provides a tranquil setting for walkers, cyclists and horse riders alike.

Northumberland National Park, which stretches from Hadrian's Wall to the Cheviot Hills. Wild and untamed, the landscapes are rich in wildlife; Kielder is the last stronghold of the red squirrel in England, with around 75 percent of the remaining population. The Northumberland National Park is also home to roe deer, otters, shrews and voles, as well as buzzards and ospreys, and the forests and hills are dotted with viewing hides.

Although the big draw here is the spectacular natural landscapes, there are also picturesque villages to explore in the nearby North Tyne valley. The tranquil feel of the area belies its violent history; the whole area was the site of many battles between the English and Scottish crowns in medieval times and again during the Jacobite rebellion in the 18th century.

Nowadays, the sleepy hamlets of Tarset, Greenhaugh and Falstone seem the very epitome of peace and quiet, surrounded by great swathes of silent conifer plantations, but the various historic ruins are proof of their military significance in centuries past.

A trip to Kielder is not for those in search of bright lights (apart from those in the skies) and late nights. For anyone from the busy south of the country, the vast open spaces of Northumberland can be something of a revelation – it is hard to believe that such wide, empty, *peaceful* spaces can still be found on our crowded island. The only thing more beautiful than these dramatic landscapes is the twinkling night sky above them, a truly spectacular, unforgettable sight.

INFORMATION

STAY The **Pheasant Inn** (01434 240382; thepheasantinn.com) in Hexham serves up fabulous slow-roasted Northumbrian lamb in a cosy dining room, and has eight comfortable bedrooms. **Kielder Lodges** (01434 251000; visitkielder.com) are luxury timber eco-chalets, from £290 per week, self-catering. **Kielder YHA** (yha.org.uk) is a great budget option; en suite family rooms from £21 per night.

EAT Meals at the **Battlesteads Inn** (01434 230209; battlesteads.com) in Hexham come with fruit, vegetables and herbs grown in the pub's own garden. Combine a trip to the Otterburn Mill with lunch at **Weavers** restaurant (01830 520225; otterburnmill.co.uk), where everything is home made.

GETTING THERE From the A69 take the B6320 to Bellingham and then the C200 (follow brown signs) to Kielder Water.

MORE INFO visitkielder.com

OTHER GREAT STARGAZING LOCATIONS
• Exmoor, Devon, England (exmoor-nationalpark.gov.uk)
• Loch Trool, Galloway Forest, Scotland (forestry.gov.uk)
• Lake Vrynwy, Wales (tourism.powys.gov.uk)

36 Take to the Water
NORFOLK BROADS, ENGLAND

Motor cruiser, barge, sailing boat or canoe – in this tranquil corner of East Anglia the only way to spend a weekend is messing about on the water.

According to Ratty, one of the much-loved characters in Kenneth Grahame's *The Wind in the Willows*, there is no greater pleasure than 'messing about on the river.' And there are few places in the UK better to mess about in than the Norfolk Broads, the country's largest protected wetlands and the third largest inland waterway. In summer the waterways teem with families and stag and hen groups but come the autumn things are quieter, and the riverbanks are tinged with gold and auburn colours.

BELOW: Messing about on boats at Horning, a picturesque village on the banks of the river Bure.

The Broads are actually shallow lakes linked by six rivers that make up a total of 200km (125 miles) of navigable and lock-free waterways. Formed in medieval times when peat was dug to use as fuel, they were flooded as the water levels rose over the centuries and there are now over 60 broads, home to a huge array of wildlife. Although the major waterways are often busy, the sheer number of broads means there is usually a quiet corner to moor up in, whether for a long sunlit lunch or a cheeky sundowner.

Most visitors to the Broads begin in Wroxham, which lies on the longest river, the Bure. Flowing for 51km (32 miles), from

ABOVE: Sunset over Filby Broad, one of the group known as Trinity Broads.

Aylsham out to the sea at Gorleston, it is the perfect place for a weekend, with plenty of moorings alongside cosy pubs and idyllic, unspoiled broads. The Bure flows into the Thurne, which gives access to Hickling Broad and Horsey Mere and picturesque villages that cling to the riverside; the lively town of Potter Heigham is particularly worth a visit.

One of the joys of a weekend on the Broads is drifting along watching the wetland wildlife. The Broads is home to the UK's largest butterfly, the swallowtail, rare dragonflies, Bewick swans and wintering

INFORMATION

STAY Richardson's Boating Holidays (0844 770 5213; richardsonsboatingholidays.co.uk) offers short breaks on boats from their boatyards in Stalham and Acle. If you're after a little on-the-water luxury, book with **Posh Boats** (01508 499167; poshboats.co.uk), which offers state-of-the art Sealine S38 motor cruisers, sleeping up to seven. If you'd rather stay on dry land and take day trips on the river, the **Black Boys Hotel** (01263 732122, blackboyshotel.co.uk) in Aylsham has five comfortable rooms above a cosy restaurant and bar

EAT One of the prettiest villages in the Broads, Ludham also has one of the best tea rooms: **Alfresco** (alfrescotearooms.co.uk) is part of a Grade II listed cottage and serves up fabulous cakes. For a classy pub meal, the **Ship Inn** (01603 270049; theshipsouthwalsham.co.uk) is a stylishly restored country pub that does fabulous weekend roasts. The **Recruiting Sergeant** (01603 737077; recruitingsergeant.co.uk) is one of the Broad's best gastropubs, with a great line in carefully prepared fish dishes.

MORE INFO enjoythebroads.com

GETTING THERE From Norwich take the A1151 to Wroxham.

OTHER GREAT BOATING HOLS
• The Kennet and Avon Canal (waterscape.com)
• The Grand Union Canal (waterscape.com)
• The Leeds and Liverpool Canal (penninewaterways.co.uk)

---

flocks of shelduck and wigeon. It's also a fisherman's dream, with perch, pike, rudd and bream gliding through the busy waters. All that's needed to fish is an Environment Agency licence, available from post offices.

Of course it is perfectly possible to enjoy the Norfolk Broads without ever taking to the water. There are 306km (190 miles) of footpaths in the area, some going through picturesque villages such as Upton and others passing through unspoiled marshland with fantastic birdwatching possibilities. For a different perspective on the landscapes, take a ride on the Bure Valley Steam Railway (bvrw.co.uk), which runs from Aylsham to Wroxham, 14km

(9 miles away). Or take a stroll around the beautiful gardens at Hoveton Hall (hovetonhallgardens.co.uk), 6ha (15 acres) that are vibrant with natural colour throughout the year.

Although many people who venture to the Broads stay on a boat, there are plenty to hire just for day trips. All manner of craft are available from canoes to motor launches to sailing boats, as well as guided boat trips offering a local's insight into the history of this unique area. Whether on the water, beside it, or in a pub garden just within sight of it, there's something particularly calming and restorative about a break in the Broads.

37 Help with the Harvest
HEREFORD, ENGLAND

Take a tour of Herefordshire's apple orchards and sample the various tastes and strengths before you indulge in a bottle or two of your favourite local cider.

England's oldest alcoholic drink has seen something of a resurgence in its fortunes in recent years. What was once the teenage tipple of choice has been reinvented as a desirable pint, with small producers cropping up across the British countryside and cider and perry festivals taking their place alongside the more established beerfests. Herefordshire has a history of cider production dating back over 350 years, and it's a great place for an autumn weekend, when visitors can join in the apple harvest and sample the different tastes and strengths.

The Cider Route (ciderroute.co.uk) is a circular trail, linking 16 cider producers, the majority of which offer tastings and enthusiastic talks about the drinks they offer. Drop into Gwatkin (gwatkincider.co.uk), where the farm shop sells their award-winning ciders by the pint as well as bottled, or book a walking tour at Sarah's Cider (sarahscider.co.uk), run by Sarah Hawkins

whose grandfather was the original creator of Scrumpy Jack. To see cider made in the original way, visit Dunkertons Mill (dunkertons.co.uk), where a 1930s traditional press is still used.

The trail circumnavigates the county town of Hereford, which makes an ideal base for an autumn weekend. Keep up the cider theme with a visit to the Cider Museum and King Offa Distillery (cidermuseum.co.uk), which charts the history of cider making from the 18th century to the present day. Take a stroll along picturesque Church Street, lined with boutiques and individual shops, before paying a visit to the town's spectacular

OPPOSITE LEFT: Herefordshire's logo is an apple, illustrating the fruit's importance to the county. RIGHT: Westons' apple orchards near the village of Much Marcle. BELOW: Hereford Cathedral and the river Wye from the Old Bridge, Hereford.

cathedral (herefordcathedral.org). There has been a place of worship on the site since Saxon times and the building is a fascinating mix of architectural styles dating from Norman times right through to the present day. The cathedral is most famous as the home of the Mappa Mundi, a medieval map of the world dating back to the 13th century.

The countryside around Hereford and the Cider Route is great for walking and cycling, with plenty of routes linking the 'black-and-white villages' for which the area is famous. Places such as Weobley, Kinnersley and Pembridge are dotted with half-timbered medieval houses that date back to the time when they were wealthy wool communities. Some of the villages are mentioned in the Domesday Book, and each one has a unique church that remains at the heart of the community.

Herefordshire is one of those counties that is often overlooked and yet it is rich in heritage and natural beauty, and pleasingly free of the hordes of visitors that flock to other regions. Whether you want a rural weekend, staying on a farm and walking or cycling between cider producers, or want to mix rural pleasures with a spot of shopping and a sophisticated billet for the night, Herefordshire can deliver plenty of both – in a delightfully relaxed, laid-back atmosphere. Just remember to pack the aspirin; cider can become addictive …

LEFT: Westons' master cider maker stands in front of two traditional oak fermenting vessels, where the apple juice remains for up to eight months until it has matured. RIGHT: The 17th-century Unicorn Inn at Weobley used to be next to an orchard that supplied fruit to make cider for the pub.

INFORMATION

STAY Book to stay in **Somerville House** (01432 273991; somervillehouse.net) in Hereford and you've all the comforts of a hotel with the warmth of a B&B – cosy lounge, superior rooms with minibar and DVD players, and stylish decor in warm caramel and chocolate tones. Stay at **Broome Farmhouse** (01989 562824; broomefarmhouse. co.uk) and you're surrounded by the apple orchards that make Broome Farm Cider – tours and tastings available, naturally. If the weather is warm enough, pitch your tent at **Lucksall Caravan & Camping Park** (01432 870213; lucksallpark.co.uk), just outside Hereford, which offers canoeing, fishing and mountain boarding.

EAT Serious foodies should head to the **Wellington** (01432 830367; wellingtonpub.co.uk), where the menu lists the local producers used and is famed for its lavish Sunday roasts. Top off a morning's shopping in Hereford with a long lunch at the **Stewing Pot** (01432 265233; stewingpot.co.uk), where the regularly changing market menu is tailored to whatever seasonal produce is available locally each day. **Gilbies** (01432 277863, gilbies.co.uk) is a fun, unpretentious bistro with a choice of tapas plates to nibble on or larger dishes for a full meal.

GETTING THERE Leave the M50 at Junction 2. Head towards Ledbury on the A417; once on the Ledbury ring road turn onto the A438 to Hereford.

MORE INFO
visitherefordshire.co.uk

OTHER CIDER HOTSPOTS
• Somerset (visitsomerset.co.uk)
• Kent (visitkent.co.uk)
• Devon (visitdevon.co.uk)

38 Go Dolphin Spotting
CARDIGAN BAY, WALES

Take a boat or simply stroll along the Ceredigion Coast Path to see dolphins playing in the Atlantic waters; gain an insight into their behaviour by visiting the Marine Wildlife Centre.

The chance to see dolphins frisking through the sea – wild rather than in captivity – is a rare treat, and even more rare in the British Isles. But there are some places that do offer a good chance of a sighting and Cardigan Bay on the west coast of Wales is one of the best; there are said to be around 200 dolphins that live in the bay. The bay stretches from Strumble Head in the south to the historic Bardsey Island in the north, but the central section – around New Quay and Aberaeron – offers the best chance of spotting dolphins.

One of the best places to stay on the bay is Aberaeron, a picturesque small town that was originally established in the 19th century as a port at the end of the Aeron River. One house in every four is listed as being either of historical or architectural interest, and it's a lovely place just to potter, with fishing boats bobbing in the harbour and wooded hills stretching away into the countryside behind. Dolphin spotting

cruises run out of Aberaeron from May to October; Seamor (07795 242445; seamor.org) run two-hour trips, while the Cardigan Bay Marine Wildlife Centre (01545 560032; cbmwc.org) runs similar trips out of New Quay.

The Centre itself is well worth a visit, with exhibitions and interactive displays that give an insight into its work of monitoring and studying bottlenose dolphins, grey seals, porpoises and other sea creatures. It's also quite possible to see the dolphins without having to take a boat trip – there are regular sightings from New Quay – although nothing quite beats watching them glide alongside your boat.

For a break from watery pursuits, head north to the town of Aberystwyth, home to the Ceredigion Museum, which is housed in a beautiful Edwardian music hall. It's also the place to climb aboard the Rheidol Railway (rheidolrailway.co.uk), which steams through a secluded wooded valley to the

RIGHT: Cardigan Bay, on the estuary of the river Teifi boasts miles of unspoiled coastline. BELOW: Bottlenose dolphins are highly sociable mammals, hunting, feeding and playing in groups, known as pods.

legendary Devil's Bridge. There are also some fabulous walks, which begin close to the station, to the Mynach Falls, Devil's Punchbowl and Jacob's Ladder.

Walkers are particularly well catered for in this part of Wales. The Ceredigion Coast Path was officially opened in 2008, linking Ynyslas in the north with the town of Cardigan in the south. The route can be split into sections, but it links some of the area's best places to visit, including National Trust properties at Penbryn Beach, Cwmtydu and Ynys Lochtyn (nationaltrust.org.uk) and the River Teifi Conservation Area.

A word of warning: there are never any guarantees of sightings, and dolphins can be surprisingly elusive. But the Cardigan Bay waters are unusually rich in wildlife and

ABOVE: Aberystwyth is the principal holiday resort of the west coast of Wales.

even if the dolphins are a no-show, there's an excellent chance of seeing seals and porpoise – as well as the spectacular Welsh coastline itself.

INFORMATION

STAY Book into **Ty Mawr Mansion** (01570 470033; tymawrmansion.co.uk) and you'll be following in the footsteps of Sienna Miller and Keira Knightley, who stayed while filming *The Edge of Love*. It might be too chilly for camping, but you can pass on the tipis and stay in a crog loft at **Forest** (01239 623633; coldatnight.co.uk) – sleek open-plan spaces in converted farm buildings. For something more conventional, the **Harbourmaster Hotel** (01545 570755; harbour-master.com) at Aberaeron is a stylish billet right on the seafront.

EAT If you love your seafood, the **Hive on the Quay** (01545 570445; hiveonthequay.co.uk) in Aberaeron is a must – home to the freshest Cardigan Bay lobster and crab, along with home-made breads and local cheeses. **Angelina's** (01758 712353; angelinas.co.uk) is a popular Italian restaurant that has a fabulous location in Abersoch on the Lleyn Peninsula. Also in Abersoch, **5 Degrees West** (01758 713788; fivedegreeswest. co.uk) is a great place to soak up the last of the autumn sunshine, with a terrace that overlooks both the bay and north to Snowdonia.

GETTING THERE Aberaeron lies on the A487.

MORE INFO
visitcardigan.com

OTHER PLACES TO SPOT DOLPHINS
• The Moray Firth, Highland
• Durleston Head, Dorset
• Gwennap Head and Lizard Point, Cornwall

39 Follow the Food Trail
RIBBLE VALLEY, ENGLAND

*Discover a hidden corner of the Lancashire countryside,
on a food-lovers tour of local producers, bakeries, shops, delis,
farms and pubs.*

Think you've never heard of the Ribble Valley? This often overlooked corner of Lancashire is actually much more familiar than many people think – although most will know it better as Middle Earth, the setting for Tolkien's famous *The Lord of the Rings* trilogy. When the author visited the area in the 1940s, he was immediately struck by the wide rivers, wooded hills and lush, misty countryside and many of the places he visited have found their way into the books.

These days the only mystical thing about the Ribble Valley is why it is so little explored. Dominated by the dramatically beautiful Forest of Bowland, the valley is home to two market towns, Clitheroe and Longridge, and 44 villages and hamlets. The Ribble Valley Food Trail is a great way to explore the area, with 30 foodie businesses to discover, from specialist ice-cream and cheese makers on rural farms to coffee

shops in Clitheroe where every cake is freshly baked each morning. As an agricultural county, food is a great way to get an insight into Lancashire life, and following the trail gives a chance to meet local producers who can offer their own

RIGHT: Cowmans Famous Sausage Shop offers 60 different varieties of sausage.

ideas as to the best ways to discover the Valley.

Autumn is the perfect time to visit, when many of the producers are reaping the harvests, and pubs such as the Inn at Whitewell (innatwhitewell.com) and the Millstone Hotel (millstonehotel.co.uk) serve up warming hotpots, casseroles and soups made from the abundant local produce. A bright autumn day is also when the area is at its most beautiful, and there are plenty of ways to explore: on horseback along the North Lancashire Bridleway, walking a stretch of the 113-km (70-mile) Ribble Way (ribbleway.co.uk), which follows the river Ribble from its source at Ribblehead to the

ABOVE: Countryside near Clitheroe.
OPPOSITE: Pendle Hill.

estuary at Preston, or on two wheels. The Valley is home to Gisburn Forest, which has some of the most challenging bike routes in the country – even experienced riders will find their knuckles turning white.

There is plenty of history to discover too. Clitheroe Castle has dominated the local landscape for over 800 years, while the dramatic escarpment of Pendle Hill is famous as the location for the Pendle Witch Trials in the 17th century. And fiction fans should follow the Tolkien Trail, a 9-km (5 ½-mile) walk starting at Stonyhurst

INFORMATION

STAY For a classic, warm B&B welcome, **Chapel Cottage** (01254 826084; chapelcottage bandb.co.uk) is a great choice, with a beautiful garden and indulgent breakfasts. Stay in the heart of the countryside at **Clough Bottom Cottages** (01254 826285; cloughbottom .co.uk), where three former farm buildings have been converted into luxury accommodation, sleeping up to eight. Staying in the countryside doesn't have to mean roughing it; **Stanley House** (01254 769200, stanleyhouse.co.uk) has 12 luxury bedrooms housed in a

Grade II listed manor house with a cutting-edge restaurant and bar.

EAT The **Three Fishes** (01254 826888; thethreefishes.com) in Mitton has been serving up food to hungry travellers for over 400 years and is a classic pub with roaring log fires and fantastic fresh fish. Gastro-tourists should try the **Northcote** (01254 240555; northcote.com), one of the best restaurants in the north-west, where the inventive menu stays true to its Lancashire roots. For a great pub meal, try **The Red Pump Inn** (01254 826227; theredpumpinn.co.uk) near Clitheroe, which serves fabulous local game.

MORE INFO
ribblevalleyfoodtrail.com

GETTING THERE From the A59 take the A671 towards Clitheroe and then the B6478 to the Ribble Valley.

OTHER FOOD TRAILS
• Gourmet Yorkshire (gourmetyorkshire.co.uk)
• Devon Food Trails (lovetheflavour.co.uk/devon-food-trails.html)
• The New Forest (thenewforest.co.uk/activities/taste-trails.aspx)

College (stonyhurst.ac.uk), where he wrote *The Lord of the Rings,* before heading out into the surrounding countryside.

But what really defines the Ribble Valley is its food – and the heritage that surrounds it. From Goosnargh cakes, baked at Tina's Corner Bakery in Longridge, to the award-winning sausages that have been made by Cowmans Butchers in Clitheroe for over a century, there is a pride that can be felt in the pubs, restaurants and shops in this corner of the north-west. Whether you follow the Food Trail or simply explore on foot or by car, you can't go far in the Ribble Valley without coming across a foodie gem – and a friendly local who wants to tell you about it.

winter

Even in the coldest months we still find reasons to be outside: browsing in Christmas markets, slithering across ice rinks, celebrating Hogmanay, dusting off the sledge for that rare fall of snow. On blue-sky days, frosted fields sparkle in the sunshine, and stretches of beach that teem with life in the summer lie quiet and tranquil. And when - and if - the snow falls, we all regress a little: tobogganing down hillsides, throwing snowballs, and delighting in the chance to see our familiar countryside reinvented in shimmering white.

40 Learn to Ice-skate
SOMERSET HOUSE, LONDON

Lace up your skates, dress warmly, and take to the ice at Somerset House, the capital's most beautiful and atmospheric outdoor rink.

Time was, ice-skating was a rare event; a one-off school holidays' treat to a crowded indoor rink, where you'd only just managed to learn to stand by the time your hour was up. Now, thanks to new technology and lower costs, outdoor rinks are ten-a-penny – but there are still few that can beat London's Somerset House (somersethouse.org.uk). The rink itself may be small, but the location is big on glamour, style and atmosphere – perfect for a Christmas treat in the capital.

Somerset House's first incarnation was as a palatial home for the Duke of Somerset. Built in 1551, at a cost of £10,000, the duke had only a year to enjoy it before being

BELOW: Somerset House provides a dramatic backdrop for London's skaters.

executed at the Tower of London and the house passed into the hands of the Crown. Oliver Cromwell lay in state at Somerset House in 1658, Christopher Wren oversaw renovations in the late 17th century and in the 18th century it became the scene of some of London's most glamorous parties. The party feel returns during ice-skating season; younger children have their own skating area, complete with push-along penguins to keep them on their feet, and there is plenty of mulled wine and hot chocolate on offer to keep non-participants warm.

Somerset House is just a couple of minutes' walk from Covent Garden market, which is at its most spectacular in the run-up to Christmas. Once the largest fruit and vegetable market in the country, it now combines boutiques, bars, an artisan market and street theatre. If the crowds become too much, a two-minute stroll will take you into the Seven Dials area, also characterized by independent shops but less of a tourist draw.

Alternatively, cross the river and walk along the newly redeveloped South Bank. Head west, and the London Eye (londoneye.com) and the impressive London Aquarium (visitsealife.com/London/) offer opposing but equally spectacular insights – over the city's rooftops or below the ocean waves. Walk east and the river route takes in the fantastic Tate Modern (tate.org.uk) in a converted former power station, and Shakespeare's Globe (shakespeares-globe.org). Further on lies London's premier address for foodies: Borough Market

INFORMATION

STAY For a truly indulgent weekend, check into the **Covent Garden Hotel** (020 7806 1000; firmdale.com), where owner Kit Kemp has created a stylish urban bolt-hole. Who says staying central has to cost a bomb? The **Premier Inn** (0871 527 8648; premierinn.com) at County Hall on the south bank has double rooms from £69. If money is no object, a short stroll along the river from Somerset House lies the **Savoy** (fairmont.com/savoy), the *grande dame* of London's hotels and plusher than ever after a recent squillion-pound refurbishment.

EAT Eating in Central London doesn't have to be pricey; try **Wahaca** (020 7240 1883; wahaca.co.uk) where plates of delicious Mexican street food cost under a fiver. Warm up with some mulled wine and nibble on traditional British cheeses at the **Crusting Pipe** (020 7836 1415, crustingpipe.co.uk) in the heart of Covent Garden market. To really push the boat out book a table at **Rules** (020 7836 5314; rules.co.uk), London's oldest restaurant (dating back to 1798) where traditional great British cooking, well, rules.

GETTING THERE Firstly, leave the car at home. Walk across the river from Waterloo Station or take the Underground Circle line to Temple station.

MORE INFORMATION visitlondon.com

OTHER GREAT RINKS
• Brighton Pavilion, Sussex (visitbrighton.com)
• Eden Project, Cornwall (edenproject.com)
• Edinburgh (edinburghschristmas.com)

ABOVE: *Covent Garden Apple Market houses around 40 stalls selling items such as antiques, craft items and handmade clothing. Fun to browse in at any time, it is particularly busy around Christmas.*

(boroughmarket.org.uk), home to dozens of stallholders selling everything from fruit and veg to specialist cheeses, meats, breads and all manner of ready-to-eat treats.

London is at its best in the run-up to Christmas; and although it can get very busy there are always quieter areas to discover. If Covent Garden is too frenetic head across the river to Gabriel's Wharf (coinstreet.org), where the artsy boutiques are a great source for Christmas presents. Alternatively, once you've slipped off your skates, head to the river and jump on a boat down to Greenwich, home to one of London's best markets. Or, if it's cold and wet, walk along the river to Embankment and find the

battered door that leads downstairs to Gordon's (gordonswinebar.com), the oldest – and quite possibly the cosiest – wine bar in London; perfect for a post-skate tipple.

41 Ski the Cairngorms
AVIEMORE, SCOTLAND

Forget flying to the Alps, stay home and discover the range of runs, pistes and half-pipes at Glenshee, the Lecht, Nevis Range and Cairngorm Mountain.

We British might not hold many medals for our skiing prowess, but the annual migration of ski-jacketed sorts to the slopes of Europe and North America makes it almost one of our national sports. Skiing *in* Britain sounds a crazy idea, but when the snow comes down, the resorts in the Cairngorms National Park offer a good choice of runs, fantastic terrain parks for boarders and cross-country, telemarking and ski touring all available from specialist operators.

Skiers have been whizzing down the slopes of Glenshee, the Lecht and Cairngorm Mountain since the 1960s and although the warmer winters of more recent years appeared to threaten the future of Scotland as a ski destination, temperatures have plummeted again in the last two and there has been excellent snowfall.

All levels of skiers and boarders are catered for at Cairngorm Mountain; the Ski School (theskischool.co.uk) offers daily and multi-day packages, with a 'Snowlimit'

programme for children, and tailored lessons in backcountry, freestyle and ski racing. Even non-skiers can enjoy the snow; the mountain has a funicular railway which runs to the peak, and the Ptarmigan Restaurant at the top is a great spot for a lazy lunch, even if you've no intention of skiing back down.

Cairngorm Mountain lies around 13km (8 miles) from the town of Aviemore, which makes an ideal base for a skiing break. It is the heart of the winter-sports scene and has lively après-ski and an excellent choice of places to stay. It also has some great places to visit if you need a day off the slopes: the Cairngorm Brewery (cairngormbrewery. com) offers the chance to taste some of the best-loved Highland Ales, while the Reindeer Centre (cairngormreindeer.co.uk)

OPPOSITE LEFT: Whitewater rafting on the river Findhorn. RIGHT: Cairngorm skiers enjoy wonderful views, such as this one of Loch Morlich. BELOW: The perfect piste.

offers the chance to meet the UK's only herd of reindeer. Kids will also love the Fun House, part of the Hilton Hotel complex but open to non-residents, which boasts soft play areas, slides, tunnels and a tree house over three floors.

Back on the pistes, if Cairngorm Mountain isn't enough of a challenge, there are other ski areas to explore within the national park. The Lecht is a great choice for families and beginners, as alongside the skiing and boarding there's also the chance to try 'tubing' – speeding down a specially groomed piste in what looks like a large inflatable rubber ring. The Lecht also has a small ski school

(school@lecht.co.uk) and all necessary equipment can be hired at the slopes.

But there is more to the Cairngorms than just shooting down the mountains as fast as possible (and slightly out of control). Those after a serious physical challenge can try ice-climbing, and if the weather has warmed up enough to melt the snow, then mountain biking, horse riding and gorge walking are all on offer. G2 Outdoor (g2outdoor.co.uk) offer a wide range of winter activities, including 'no-snow alternatives' such as rafting or hiking. Snow may not always be guaranteed, but a stay in the Cairngorms will be an unforgettable experience, whatever the weather.

INFORMATION

STAY The **Hilton Coylumbridge** (01479 810661; hilton.co.uk) is just the place to soothe those post-piste aches and pains, with an indoor pool and sauna, and luxurious rooms. **Pine Bank Chalets** (01479 810000; pinebankchalets.co.uk) have a fittingly alpine feel; comfortable wood cabins that are toasty in winter and sleep 2–6. For a budget ski break, **Rosegrove Guesthouse** (01479 851335; rosegroveguesthouse.com) is ideally located near to Cairngorm Mountain, and serves up a hearty breakfast to get you going in the morning.

EAT The **Ptarmigan Restaurant** (01479 861336) is the highest restaurant in the UK, at 1,097m (3,540ft) above sea level, at the top station of the Cairngorm Mountain Railway. The **Cas Bar** (01479 861261) is the perfect post-piste hang-out, situated at the bottom of the mountain with roaring log fires and fabulous home-made soups. In cold weather, comfort food is called for and the bowls of pasta and warming pizza at **La Taverna** (01479 810683; highrange.co.uk) in Aviemore are guaranteed to hit the spot.

GETTING THERE From the A9 Aviemore road, take the B970 road signed to Cairngorm Mountain and follow for 11km (7 miles).

MORE INFO
ski.visitscotland.com

OTHER PLACES TO SKI
• Glenshee, Scotland (ski-glenshee.co.uk)
• Yad Moss, Cumbria (yadmoss.co.uk)
• Nevis Range, Scotland (nevisrange.co.uk)

42
Spot the Snowdrops
HOWICK, ENGLAND

Celebrate the first signs of spring with a visit to one of Northumberland's most beautiful gardens in the grounds of 18th-century Howick Hall.

There are few more cheering sights in the cold winter months than the sight of the first snowdrops poking up through the frosty soil; neat clusters of white blooms that hint at the possibility of winter slowly starting to recede. Howick Hall (howickhallgardens.com) in Britain's rural north-east corner, is one of the best places in the country to see winter snowdrops, with an annual Snowdrop Festival every February The snowdrops were originally planted between the wars, and flower in large drifts across the gardens.

Howick is steeped – quite literally – in British history; the ancestral home of the Earls Grey – and former home of the prime minister, Earl Charles Grey, after whom the tea was named. Owned by the Grey family since the 14th century, the current house dates back to the 18th century, and is not open to the public, as it remains a private

residence. The spectacular grounds, however, are open all year – from snowdrop walks in February, a wild bog garden and borders at their peak in summer, right through to spectacular autumn colours.

RIGHT: Snowdrop fanciers or galanthophiles are in for a treat at Howick Hall gardens.

The garden includes woodland, herbaceous borders and rockeries and a bog garden that is home to many exotic plants. Howick is also famous as one of the few places left in Britain where red squirrels can be seen – there are feeders outside the tea-room windows that offer the chance to see them up close.

For garden lovers, this area of the country is the perfect place for a weekend break, as the famous Alnwick Garden (alnwickgarden.com) is just a short drive from Howick. Until 10 years ago, the site was derelict, and the gardens have slowly been created by the Duchess of Northumberland. The ambitious project has created different areas of garden, from ornamental to a 'poison' garden, with fountains for children to play in, a tree-house restaurant and a staggering variety of plants and trees. A visit to the garden can be twinned with a visit to Alnwick Castle (alnwickcastle.com), a stunning medieval castle that will be familiar from its roles in the Harry Potter films and the Blackadder series.

The other big draw for visitors to Northumberland is the dramatic coastline which stretches south from Berwick-upon-Tweed past Howick, with long stretches of sandy beaches, dominated by spectacular fortresses such as Bamburgh Castle and Holy Island. In winter, if the skies are blue, the coastal scenery is at its most beautiful – and the beaches are often deserted, giving them a slightly haunted feeling.

ABOVE: Alnwick Garden is stunning at any time of the year. OPPOSITE: Bamburgh Castle from Seahouses.

The villages of the Northumberland coast have a very particular charm, from pretty Bamburgh to sleepy Seahouses, right on the beach, that looks across to the Farne Islands. Famous for the colonies of birds and seals which make the islands their home, there are regular wildlife-spotting boat trips (farne-islands.com) from Seahouses. The combination of spectacular gardens, dramatic coastline and a rich history makes this corner of Northumberland the perfect weekend break.

INFORMATION

STAY It might be a bit chilly for camping, but **Springhill Farm** (01665 721820; springhill-farm.co.uk) also offers cottages and fully insulated wooden wigwams in a spectacular location with lovely sea views. In the heart of Alnwick, **Blackmores** (01665 602395; blackmoresofalnwick.com) has 13 luxurious rooms above one of the town's best restaurants. Just outside Bamburgh, **Budle Hall** (01668 214297; budlehall.co.uk) is a small, elegant country house that offers a touch of grandeur to a traditional B&B stay.

EAT Lunch at the **Treehouse** at Alnwick Garden (01665 511852; alnwickgarden.com) is an experience not to be missed; high in the treetops with a roaring log fire, it's the perfect winter restaurant. In Bamburgh, the **Copper Kettle Tearooms** (01668 214315; copperkettletearooms. com) is legendary for its home-made pies and cakes. Sometimes there's nothing to beat hot fish and chips, and **Carlos** (01665 602787; carlosfishandchips.co.uk), in Alnwick, is generally agreed to be one of the best chippies in the whole of Northumberland.

GETTING THERE Leave the A1 for the B1339 and follow the signs to Longhoughton. Once through the village follow the signs to Howick.

MORE INFO
visitnorthumberland.com

OTHER SNOWDROP WALKS
• Snowdrop Valley, Exmoor, Devon (exmoor.com)
• Painswick Rococo Garden, Gloucestershire (rococogarden.co.uk)
• Anglesey Abbey, Cambridgeshire (nationaltrust.org.uk)

43 Shop Till You Drop
LINCOLN, ENGLAND

Indulge in a mulled-wine-fuelled shopping spree around England's oldest and biggest Christmas market in Lincolnshire's historic cathedral city.

There's been something of an explosion in Christmas markets in recent years; come the first week of December, most major towns across the country take on a distinctly Germanic feel, with wooden huts selling gingerbread and the air thick with the smell of Glühwein and sizzling bratwurst. But there's nothing new about Lincoln's Christmas shenanigans; the city is home to the oldest and best-loved Christmas market in the UK, and the varied stalls – home to local craftsmen, artists, jewellery makers and artisan food producers – offer great potential for unusual Christmas gifts.

The market usually takes place on the first weekend of December, and has gone from 11 stalls in 1982 to 250, all situated around the medieval marketplace and the cobbled streets of the old town. As well as the market, there are live music performances on each of the four days, from classical to carol singing and rock bands, and traditional events such as barrel rolling also take place. A word of caution: over a quarter of a million people visit for the market and it does get incredibly busy – getting there early is a good idea.

Aside from the market, there is much to discover in Lincoln. Often overlooked as a weekend destination, the city is one of the UK's most historic – and beautiful. No visit is complete without seeing the awe-inspiring cathedral (lincolncathedral.com), described by John Ruskin as 'the most precious piece of architecture in the British Isles'. Towering above the city, the cathedral is visible from 40km (25 miles) away and has been a place of worship for over 1,000 years, famous for its beautiful stained-glass windows and 14th-century stone carvings.

RIGHT: The floodlit front of Lincoln Cathedral provides a spectacular backdrop to the hustle and bustle of the Christmas market in the medieval square and adjacent streets.

Equally impressive is Lincoln Castle, originally built by William the Conqueror and one of the most complete remaining Norman castles in the country. Kids will love the chance to clamber up onto the walls and explore the 900-year-old rooms that were once used as prison cells. The castle is also home to one of the four remaining copies of the Magna Carta. Also worth seeing is the medieval Bishop's Palace, once one of the most important buildings in the country. In between all the history, there is plenty to discover in 21st-century Lincoln; the Brayford waterfront is an ideal spot for lunch, with buzzy restaurants and bars lining the promenade.

Lincoln is also rich in aviation history (aviationlincolnshire.com); known as Bomber County in the Second World War because of the airbases located in the area, RAF Scampton is the present-day home of the Red Arrows, and visitors to the region are often treated to a practice display in the wide, Lincolnshire skies. Scampton is also home to a historical museum dedicated to the legendary Dambusters. For something more peaceful, Hartsholme (hartsholmecountrypark.com) is an elegant country park and lake that offers the chance of a relaxing stroll – perfect after the hustle and bustle of the busy market streets.

INFORMATION

STAY Located in the Uphill area of the city, the **Old Bakery** (01522 576057; theold-bakery.co.uk) is a delightful restaurant with four cosy rooms upstairs. Indulge in the seven-course tasting menu, secure in the knowledge it's only a short few stairs up to bed. To soak up some of the town's rich history, stay at the **Bail House Hotel** (01522 541000; bailhouse.co.uk), which dates back to 1350 and offers comfortable rooms and self-catering cottages in the Bailhouse Mews. Combine a rural stay with a Christmas shopping spree, at **Bardney Manor Cottage**, midway between Lincoln and the Wolds; one of many cottages in the area available through Hoseasons (0844 847 1115; hoseasons.co.uk).

EAT In the heart of the city, **Gino's** (01522 513770; ginoslincoln.co.uk) is a great place for lunch, with a wide range of authentic Italian dishes and a wonderful line in indulgent desserts. **The Swan Holme** (01522 509859; vintageinn. co.uk/theswanholmelincoln/) is a traditional pub just outside the city that offers good-sized portions of comfort food in a warm, welcoming atmosphere. The **Jews House** (01522 524851; jewshouserestaurant.co.uk) is an ideal choice for an upscale dinner, with beautifully presented, subtle dishes.

MORE INFO visitlincoln.com

GETTING THERE Lincoln is accessed from the A1 by the A57 (north) and the A46 (south).

OTHER GREAT CHRISTMAS MARKETS
• York (visityork.org)
• Winchester (visitwinchester.co.uk)
• Bath (visitbath.co.uk)

44 Pick a Pub
DERBY, ENGLAND

Let your hair down and go on a pub crawl around this revitalized East Midlands city, where real ale rules and there are over 100 great hostelries to choose from.

When it's cold, grey and windy outside there are few better places to be than a cosy British pub. As much a part of the national psyche as Marmite toast and *Coronation Street*, pubs have been an

BELOW LEFT: Ye Olde Dolphin Inn is Derby's oldest pub. BELOW RIGHT: The Derwent Valley Mills combined water power with new mechanized processes to revolutionize textile production in Britain.

integral part of the British way of life for centuries; something that shows little sign of changing. Our definition of a pub may have changed – many now offer great food, comfortable bedrooms, brew their own beer or grow their own ingredients – but all good pubs should offer the same three basic qualities: a warm welcome, good beer and a cosy atmosphere.

For pub aficionados on a weekend break there is no better place to visit than Derby, recently recommended by the *Good Pub Guide* as having some of the best pubs in the country. The city has proudly awarded itself the title of 'Real Ale Capital of the Midlands', and with over 120 real-ale pubs, and several microbreweries within the city, it's a fair claim. Pubs such as the Brunswick Inn (1 Railway Terrace), Ye Olde Dolphin Inn (5a Queen Street), the Flowerpot (23–25 King St) and the Falstaff (74 Silver Hill Rd) are all within walking distance and offer well-kept beers and friendly staff who are happy to pass on their knowledge of the local area.

Although perhaps not an obvious choice for a weekend break, there is a surprising amount to see and do in Derby. In the 18th and 19th centuries the city flourished, with its silk and cotton mills at the heart of the Industrial Revolution. It also became a centre for the railway industry, and there are many heritage sites dotted around the city,

BELOW: At night, the dramatic frontage of the Quad, Derby's community art centre, forms a striking contrast with its neighbour, the historic Guildhall Market. During the day its natural stone cladding blends in pleasingly.

INFORMATION

STAY If you need a drop of luxury to make the hangover bearable, the **Cathedral Quarter Hotel** (01332 546080; cathedralquarterhotel.com) has luxurious bedrooms and a Clink Spa for restorative therapies. If you can get past the name, **Chuckles Guesthouse** (01332 367193; chucklesguesthouse.co.uk) is a good value B&B that does a great veggie breakfast. For something different, the **Millhouse Derby** (0845 122 0405; sacoapartments.co.uk) offers serviced, luxury, one- and two-bed apartments with excellent self-catering facilities and fabulous views over the city.

EAT Graze (01332 208262; grazerestaurant.co.uk) is a carnivore's dream, with locally sourced steaks and burgers on the grill, and hearty pies and pot roasts. If you've peaked on pubs, drop into **No 5** (01332 343250; numberfive.co.uk), a cosy bar offering live jazz in the evening, and good baguettes and plates of cold meats and cheeses to share. For a romantic dinner *à deux*, local favourite **Restaurant Zest** (01332 381101; restaurantzest.co.uk) serves excellent seasonal dishes and fabulous indulgent puds.

MORE INFO visitderby.co.uk

GETTING THERE Leave the M1 at junction 25 and follow the A52 to Derby.

OTHER GREAT CITY PUB CRAWLS
• Rose Street, Edinburgh (Edinburgh.org)
• Brighton, East Sussex (visitbrighton.com)
• The Canton Mile, Cardiff (visitcardiff.com)

---

including the Silk Mill, which give an insight into Derby's industrial heritage, and the Derwent Valley Mills (derwentvalleymills.org) – a UNESCO World Heritage Site, which stretches for 24km (15 miles) along the river from Derby to Matlock.

The city has reinvented itself in recent years, and has a pleasingly contemporary feel with new venues such as the Quad (derbyquad.co.uk), which combines a cinema, art gallery, cafe and workshop in an architecturally impressive space. For those who like to shop, Westfield Derby is a gleaming new shopping centre with 175 stores and regular events taking place inside the space.

One of the joys of Derby is that there is plenty of green space to explore alongside the busy streets – Derby Arboretum is the first and oldest surviving public park in England and is ideal for a blustery winter stroll to blow the (post-pub) cobwebs away. One of the best times to visit the city in the winter is in the weeks before Christmas, when the picturesque cathedral quarter is decked out in fairy lights and the individual boutiques have a fantastic range of gifts. The city streets are at their busiest in the pre-Christmas weeks, but there is one reassuring thought – with 120 proper pubs to chose from, you'll always be sure of finding a seat.

45 Celebrate Hogmanay
EDINBURGH, SCOTLAND

Take to the streets for the biggest party in the country, as Scotland's most vibrant city celebrates New Year in unforgettable style.

On 31 December there are New Year's Eve celebrations, and then there are New Year's Eve *celebrations*. Edinburgh falls firmly into the second category – Scotland's capital city is arguably the prime party spot for the evening of the 31st, with street parties, fireworks, bands and enough general shenanigans to fill four whole days. Hogmanay, as it is known in Scotland, is about more than just the one night – the party can last for as long as your stamina can hold out.

Hogmanay celebrations are believed to have originated from the Vikings, who invaded Scotland in the early 8th and 9th

BELOW: Fireworks and festive lighting enhance the already beautiful city skyline.

centuries; they celebrated it as the winter solstice – the shortest day of the year. The turn of the year remained the biggest celebration in the Scottish calendar right up until the 20th century; during the Protestant Reformation of the 17th century, Christmas as a festival was practically banned, and even in the 1950s many Scots had to work through Christmas and so saved the celebrations for New Year's Eve.

To celebrate Hogmanay in Edinburgh, it's important to be aware of the tradition of 'first-footing'. New Year's Eve is a night when many Scots open up their homes, and from midnight onwards people are welcomed into each other's houses, bringing gifts such as whisky, shortbread and 'black bun' – a rich fruitcake. Invitations are often offered freely and it's a great way to meet some local people and take part in one of Scotland's most longstanding traditions.

Aside from the partying, there is much to see and do in Edinburgh. The city centre is a UNESCO World Heritage site (ewht.org.uk), combining the medieval Old Town, the Georgian New Town and some stunning architecture. The best place to start exploring is a walk along the Royal Mile, which stretches from Edinburgh Castle to the Palace of Holyroodhouse and has been a processional route for monarchs for over 500 years. The route is dotted with historic buildings, including the 12th-century cathedral, a 17th-century tenement and the house of Protestant reformer John Knox.

For a spot of shopping and a lazy lunch head to Grassmarket, one of the oldest parts of the city, and a marketplace for centuries. Dotted with independent shops and boutiques, it's also home to possibly the oldest pub in the city, the White Hart Inn. The climb of 142 steps to the top of the Scott Monument in Princes Street Gardens is worth it for the fantastic panorama across the city's rooftops. Dean Village is a tranquil oasis with period houses and old water mills set on the banks of the Water of Leith. Just five minutes' walk from bustling Princes Street, it is a perfect example of the different ways to experience this historic city.

BELOW: Edinburgh's famous skyline on a bright winter's day.

INFORMATION

STAY Edinburgh has a host of stylish hotels, but none more so than the **Missoni** (0131 220 6666; hotelmissoni.com), created by the famous Italian design house and currently the city's hippest address. If you don't want the party to end, **Le Monde** (0131 270 3900; lemondehotel.co.uk) is the perfect choice, with three bars and the Shanghai Club – one of Edinburgh's top nightclubs. If you'd rather stay a little away from the mayhem, the **Sun Inn** (0131 663 2456; thesuninneskbank.co.uk), on the outskirts of the city, has five luxury rooms above a cosy bar and more formal dining room.

EAT After a heavy night, sometimes only a slap-up breakfast will do, and **Urban Angel** (0131 225 6215; urban-angel.co.uk) serves up fabulous Eggs Benedict and local sausages and bacon. For a tea-and-cake stop in the middle of a shopping spree, visit **Peter's Yard** (0131 228 5876; petersyard.co.uk), which serves up scrummy muffins and pastries along with fresh salads and sandwiches. For a top-end dinner, **21212** (21212restaurant.co.uk) offers flawless modern French cookery in an elegantly converted, listed Georgian town house.

MORE INFO
edinburghshogmanay.com

GETTING THERE There are good flight links from regional airports to Edinburgh; by car it is accessed from the A720 Edinburgh bypass.

OTHER GREAT NEW YEAR'S EVE CELEBRATIONS
• Cardiff, Wales (visitcardiff.com)
• London (london.gov.uk/ newyearseve)
• Newcastle (newcastlegateshead.com/ winterfestival)

46 Forage for Fossils
CHARMOUTH, ENGLAND

Take the kids and uncover millions of years of history as you potter along the beaches of Dorset's spectacular Jurassic Coast, searching the sands and cliffs for new discoveries.

Geology. It's not the most dramatic of subjects – rocks, strata, minerals – and most of the time it's an area of knowledge where the evidence is hidden from sight. An exception is the West Country's breathtaking Jurassic Coast, which stretches for 153 km (95 miles) from East Devon to Dorset, charting the physical development of our island home over 185 million years. England's first natural World Heritage Site, the sheer cliffs and layered rocks provide a dramatic backdrop to stunning beaches, great walks and the region's favourite pastime – fossil hunting.

The cliffs that line this part of the coast are rich in the fossilized remains of animals that swam in the sea during the Jurassic period, with the small towns of Charmouth and Lyme Regis particularly good hunting grounds. The winter months, when storms whip up the sand and stones and lash the cliffs, are the best time for fossil hunting and you can either simply potter around on your own or take a guided Fossil Walk (fossilwalks.com).

In summer the beaches teem with visitors but in winter there is a tranquillity to be found among the dramatic landscapes that date back hundreds of millennia. On a crisp winter's day the walk up onto Golden Cap – at 191m (626ft) the highest point on the South Coast – offers spectacular views, and the South West Coast Path (southwestcoastpath.com) stretches on towards the pretty village of Seatown and the market town of Bridport. The Golden Cap estate is National Trust-owned and has 40km (25 miles) of paths through woods and farmland on the cliff top.

Charmouth is a charming small town, with an excellent Heritage Centre

OPPOSITE ABOVE LEFT: What will the hammer reveal? RIGHT: A rooftop view of Lyme Regis. BELOW: Charmouth Beach and Golden Cap cliff.

(charmouth.org/chcc) that has displays on the geology and history of the region and also organizes walks and events throughout the year. The high street is dotted with old-fashioned gift shops and cafes offering hot pasties and cream teas, and the pace of life is pleasingly slow.

Nearby Lyme Regis, made famous by the film *The French Lieutenant's Woman*, is a bustling former fishing port, with a charming old town that dates back to the 14th century. The high street, dotted with art galleries, delicatessens and gift shops, slopes sharply down to the sandy beach below. Head east, in the opposite direction to Lyme, and it's just a short drive to the charming town of Bridport, best visited on a Saturday morning when the market is in full swing, selling everything from antiques to plants and home-made bread.

One of the great joys of this part of the world – even on a rainy winter's day – is turning the car off the main road and disappearing into the lattice of B roads that link medieval villages and hamlets and cosy country pubs. Names such as Wootton Fitzpaine, Fishpond Bottom and Whitechurch Canonicorum appear on old-fashioned signposts, and all signs of 21st-century life slip away. There's nothing to do but glide slowly up and down the lush hills until you happen upon a thatched-roof pub, with a roaring fire and a nice line in warming reds. Perfect.

INFORMATION

STAY Less than 90m (100 yards) from Charmouth beach, **Swansmead B&B** (01297 560465; swansmead.co.uk) is a great bet for families, with a family room that sleeps four and a double en suite. **Abbots House** (01297 560339; abbotshouse.co.uk) is a stylish guest house that dates back to medieval times and has been tastefully restored, with four rooms that boast flatscreen TVs, DVDs and indulgently luxurious bathrooms. **Wood Farm** (01297 561243; woodfarm.co.uk) is a beautifully landscaped caravan and camping site, with on-site shop.

EAT The restaurant at the **White House Hotel** (01297 560411; whitehousehotel.com) specializes in local produce – Lyme Bay seafood and fish, meats from nearby farms and hand-made cheeses. Twin a stroll around Lyme Regis with a stop for a cream tea at the **Mill Tea & Dining Room** (01297 445757; teaanddiningroom.com) where everything is home made on the premises. In nearby Bridport the **Bull Hotel** (01308 422878; thebullhotel.co.uk) is a 17th-century coaching inn renovated into a stylish gastropub.

GETTING THERE Follow the A35 – east from Axminster or west from Bridport. At the roundabout with the A3052 take the minor road signposted Charmouth.

MORE INFO charmouth.org

OTHER FOSSIL-HUNTING AREAS
• Kimmeridge, Dorset (jurassiccoast.com)
• The Brora River, Sutherland (northhighlandsscotland.com)
• Dunrobin, Sutherland (northhighlandsscotland.com)

47 Have a Spooky Weekend
WHITBY, ENGLAND

Soak up the Gothic atmosphere of this Yorkshire fishing town, the inspiration behind Bram Stoker's Dracula, *and treat yourself to some of the best fish and chips in the country.*

Few towns offer as much in such a small package as Whitby: picturesque cobbled streets lined with boutiques and brasseries, a busy harbour with a working fishing fleet, a sandy beach and, overlooking it all, the spectacular ruins of the 13th-century abbey, steeped in history and lending a touch of Gothic horror to this vibrant seaside resort. Recently named the UK's most romantic ruin, the abbey was originally founded in AD657 by St Hilda, and is said to have been the inspiration behind Bram Stoker's popular novel, *Dracula*.

The abbey dominates the town, and the legends that surround Stoker – including that he used to sleep in the graveyard of the tiny St Mary's Church – all feed into the Gothic feel. At night, the twisty dark lanes that run between the former fishermen's cottages feel exactly like a location in Stoker's novel, and

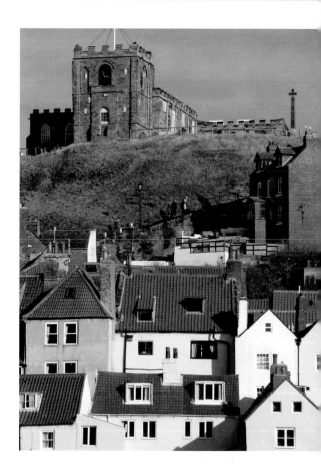

RIGHT: Whitby's colourful houses form a striking contrast with the exterior of St Mary's Church.

those in search of chills and thrills can join a Whitby Ghost Walk (whitbywalks.com), which departs at 8 p.m. most evenings.

By day, however, the town has a bright and breezy feel, with a buzzing harbour front and a tangle of cobbled streets that house quirky shops selling Whitby jet, bespoke jewellery, homewares and, of course, plenty of Dracula-themed souvenirs. Self-catering is a great option in Whitby, as there are so many specialist foodie shops – fish lovers should drop into Fortunes Kippers on Henrietta Street for some of the best kippers in Britain.

The town is also famous for its maritime links, as the famous explorer Captain James Cook came to serve his apprenticeship in Whitby in 1746. The 17th-century

harbourside house where he lived is now a museum (cookmuseumwhitby.co.uk), which has an impressive exhibition of artefacts and memorabilia from the life of Yorkshire's most famous son. On a rainy winter's day, Whitby Museum (whitbymuseum.org.uk) is also well worth a visit, with a collection of fossils and jet, along with ship models and maps dating back to Captain Cook's time.

Whitby is an ideal place to combine coast and country, as it is located on the western edge of the North Yorks National Park. Villages such as Egton, Danby and Ainthorpe have an unspoiled, rural charm and are the starting point for some pleasant, gentle walks into the countryside. Danby is home to the Moors Centre, (northyorkmoors.org.uk), a visitor centre for the national park on the banks of the river Esk, with a great play area for the kids and plenty of information about the park itself.

But one of the greatest pleasures in Whitby has to be one of the simplest: eating hot fish and chips straight from the paper whilst sitting gazing out to sea. Best of all there's an easy way to work them off – it's 199 steps up to the abbey from the old town, and if you climb them at night the spooky atmosphere is bound to have you running straight down again, back to the reassuring buzz and warmth of the town.

LEFT: The Magpie Cafe is well known for its fish and chips. RIGHT: The fishing village of Staithes, near Whitby.

INFORMATION

STAY The **White Horse and Griffin** (01947 604857; whitehorseandgriffin.co.uk) makes a great base in the heart of Whitby, with 10 cosy bedrooms above a sleek restaurant serving up plenty of Yorkshire beef and locally caught fish. The town's hippest address is currently the **Marine Hotel** (01947 605022; the-marine-hotel.co.uk), situated on the harbour with four indulgently elegant rooms and a bright, modern restaurant with a menu that changes daily. **Explorer's Rest** is a comfortably furnished town house in the centre of Whitby, sleeping up to eight; just one of a collection of self-catering cottages available through Whitby Cottages (01947 603010; whitbyholidaycottages.net).

EAT A Whitby institution, the **Magpie Cafe** (01947 602058; magpiecafe.co.uk) specializes in local fish and seafood dishes, and is famous for its chowder and spectacular fish and chips. **Botham's of Whitby** (01947 602823; botham.co.uk) has been serving up tea and home-made cakes since 1865, and is the best place in town to try Yorkshire Brack – a rich fruitcake. The **Fox and Hounds** (01947 893372; foxandhoundsgoldsborough.co.uk) is a short drive out of town, but worth it for the spectacular and innovative cooking.

INFO discoveryorkshirecoast.com

GETTING THERE Whitby lies on the A171, north of Scarborough and south of Middlesborough.

OTHER SPOOKY PLACES
• Culloden Moor, Inverness. (nts.org.uk)
• Highgate Cemetery, London (highgate-cemetery.org)
• Pendle Hill, Lancashire (visitlancashire.com)

48 Travel Back in Time
LAVENHAM, ENGLAND

Stroll the streets of the most complete medieval village in Britain, tucked away in the tranquil Suffolk countryside, and pop into its many antique shops and art galleries.

Every so often you stumble across a corner of England that reassures you the place hasn't changed so very much in the last few decades. Lavenham, tucked away in deepest Suffolk, is just that kind of place: a picturesque high street dotted with small, independent shops where people not only say hello but actually *smile*. There is no Starbucks glinting on the corner, no Tesco Metro or Pizza Express. Instead, charmingly wonky half-timbered buildings house antique shops, bespoke jewellers and art galleries. In Lavenham people don't stride or jog, frantically prodding their Blackberries, they *potter*.

Pottering around Lavenham has to be one of the nicest ways to spend an afternoon Christmas shopping. The town is steeped in

LEFT The medieval Crooked House is now home to an art gallery. It was built by a rich cloth merchant around 1395 as the service wing of his grand house.

heritage: 500 years ago it was the 14th wealthiest in England, thanks to a booming wool industry that created wealthy merchants who built impressive homes. That so many have survived for half a millennium is almost miraculous, and although many of them lean and stoop – as befits their great age – they still house private homes, businesses and even cafes and restaurants.

The best place to start in Lavenham is on the historic Market Place, with a quick visit to the NT-owned Guildhall, which has exhibits on the town's history. Dating back to about 1530, it is still used as a hub of village activities, although Harry Potter fans may be more familiar with it as the home of the boy wizard's parents in the latest films. Once you've absorbed the history, step back out into the main square and simply soak up the atmosphere. Every street is a jumble of half-timbered antique homes and more modern cottages – it all adds to the higgledy-piggledy charm.

ABOVE FAR LEFT AND LEFT: Visitors to Lavenham should allow enough time to notice the many lovely architectural details of its famous medieval buildings, such as the overhanging beams of the Crooked House and the carvings flanking the Guildhall entrance.
BELOW LEFT: Medieval house on the corner of Market Lane and High Street.
OPPOSITE: Lavenham's famous Guildhall was built as a meeting place for the Guild of Corpus Christi, a small but powerful group of businessmen and gentry. It has had many uses since then and is now a museum and performance venue.

In the winter months, under a crisp blue sky, Lavenham is at its most charming. Shops lure you in with the promise of unusual gifts: handmade jewellery at Moi (70 Water St), locally made ceramics and artworks at the Crooked House Gallery (7 High St), chic bags, hats and shoes at Vintage Pink (22 High St) and beautiful landscapes by local artist Paul Evans at Lavenham Contemporary (70–71 High St). And don't miss Timbers Antiques, also on the high street, an apparently small shop that opens out into an Aladdin's Cave of vintage goodies.

If you want to explore beyond Lavenham, the surrounding area is rich in history. Long Melford is a charming village dotted with antique shops and home to two imposing Elizabethan mansions: Melford Hall (nationaltrust.org.uk/melfordhall), which has vast grounds, perfect for a brisk winter walk, and Kentwell Hall (kentwell.co.uk), famous for its historic recreation weekends.

Walkers are well served: there is a well-trodden 5-km (3.1-mile) walk around Lavenham, and a 6-km (3.7-mile) trail to Long Melford – maps for both are available at the tourist office in Market Place. Art lovers should drop into the pretty market town of Sudbury, childhood home of Thomas Gainsborough. The house where Gainsborough grew up is now an art gallery, with more of his work on display than anywhere else in the world.

INFORMATION

STAY **Lavenham Cottages** (01787 249423; lavenhamcottages.co.uk) are four luxury cottages on the historic Market Place, sleeping up to four. The most famous billet in town is the **Swan Hotel** (01787 247477; theswanatlavenham.co.uk), three spectacular medieval houses melded together (the oldest part dates back to the 14th century) to create a luxurious hotel. The **Great House** (01787 247431; greathouse.co.uk) is one of Suffolk's most renowned restaurants, with chic bedrooms above that look out over Market Place.

EAT If you're celebrating, or feel like a splurge, the **Great House** (as above) offers cooking that is as sophisticated as its rooms. Just across the square lies the **Angel Hotel** (01284 714000; theangel.co.uk), where the lively bar is filled with locals and serves up great pub food. For a mid-shopping restorative lunch, or indulgent slab of cake, drop into **Munnings** on the High Street (munningstearoom.com).

GETTING THERE Leave the M11 at junction 8a. Take the A120 east to Braintree, followed by the A131 to Sudbury. From Sudbury take the B1115 to Great Waldingfield, then the left fork onto the B1071 to Lavenham.

MORE INFO visit-suffolk.org.uk

OTHER MEDIEVAL TOWNS
• Sandwich, Kent (open-sandwich.co.uk)
• Norwich, Norfolk (visitnorwich.co.uk)
• Castle Combe, Wiltshire (castle-combe.com)

49 Glam It Up
BURGH ISLAND, ENGLAND

Follow in the footsteps of Agatha Christie and enjoy an indulgent weekend in this Devonshire island retreat, where good old-fashioned glamour still reigns.

There's nothing like a splash of good old-fashioned glamour to cheer up a chilly winter weekend, and the Burgh Island Hotel has it in spades. Originally built in 1929, the hotel has retained its art deco architecture and decor, and a stay there is an unforgettable mix of contemporary luxury and 1930s style. Burgh Island is most famous for its links with Agatha Christie, who stayed on the island several times and wrote (and set) two of her novels there: *Evil Under the Sun* and *And Then There Were None*. It is also notorious as a bolt-hole for Edward and Mrs Simpson, who spent long afternoons on the island in the run-up to the abdication crisis.

Burgh Island is not about slobbing around in jeans and trainers; black tie and evening dresses are required on Saturday nights, when an old-fashioned dinner dance takes place in the dining room. More informal dining is on offer at the Pilchard Inn, a 14th-century smugglers' pub that is also on the island, and there's plenty of relaxing to be done with a good menu of in-room spa treatments.

One of the most unique things about a stay on Burgh Island is the chance to ride on the world's only sea tractor; basically an elevated cage on wheels that carries guests to the island from Bigbury when the tide is in. At low tide it is possible to walk across, although a ride on the tractor shouldn't be missed – not least because its elevated position is the perfect place to spot the groups of seals that are often seen gliding through the waters around the island.

On the mainland, there is plenty to see and do. Even on a wintry day the beach at Bigbury – the village directly opposite Burgh Island – is inviting; a wide expanse of sand that gleams beneath a sharp, blue winter's sky, backed by low cliffs on one side and the estuary of the river Avon on the

RIGHT: At low tide Bigbury and Burgh Island are connected by a strip of sand.

ABOVE: Burgh Island Hotel.

other. The village is at the heart of South Hams, a beautiful part of Devon that mixes small coastal resorts such as Salcombe and Totnes with larger towns such as Dartmouth and tranquil rolling countryside.

Dartmouth (discoverdartmouth.com) makes a great day out from Burgh Island: narrow medieval streets dotted with boutiques and gift shops, a spectacular castle that has guarded the entrance to the Dart Estuary for over 600 years (english-heritage.org) and river-boat trips that leave the coast behind and head up into the hills. Alternatively it's easy to explore this stretch of coastline on foot: the South West Coast Path offers a mix of spectacular cliffs and picturesque villages. However you spend your days, a weekend at Burgh Island will guarantee a real sense of escape – not just to a different place, but to a different time.

INFORMATION

STAY Whether you book a themed murder weekend or just a romantic night à deux, **Burgh Island** (01548 810514; burghisland.com) is an unforgettable experience. If it's a little too pricey however, try the **Henley Hotel** (01548 810240; car-mod-shop.co.uk/ henleyhotel) just across the water on the mainland, a former holiday cottage with cosy rooms and a great restaurant that looks out directly over the water. The **Royal Oak** (01548 810313; theroyaloakbigbury.com) is a great bet for a cosy winter stay, with sleek bedrooms above a dining room specializing in fresh fish and local meats.

EAT If you decide not to stay on the island (or even if you do) pop across to the **Pilchard Inn** (burghisland.com/pilchard.html), where a pint and a plate of oysters make the perfect lunch. Back on the mainland, there are few better places in England for fresh seafood than the South Devon coast; tuck into all manner of molluscs at the **Oyster Shack** (01548 810876; oystershack.co.uk) in Bigbury. The **Bay View** cafe (01548 810796) is renowned for serving up some of best cream teas in the area – not to be missed.

GETTING THERE From the A379 follow the B3392 through Bigbury and on to Bigbury-on-Sea.

MORE INFO burghisland.com

OTHER CHRISTIE-RELATED HOTELS
• Imperial Hotel, Torquay (barcelo-hotels.co.uk)
• Old Swan Hotel, Harrogate (macdonaldhotels.co.uk)
• Brown's Hotel, London (brownshotel.com)

50 Watch the Birdies
SNETTISHAM, ENGLAND

See the vast skies above Norfolk come alive as wintering birds swoop and swarm in their thousands, or watch the wading birds retreat from their feeding grounds as the tide comes in.

You don't have to be a twitcher to marvel at the spectacle of tens of thousands of birds gathering on the vast expanses of the Wash. It is an astonishing sight; at dusk or dawn in the winter months, thousands of Pink-footed Geese can be seen flying from their overnight roost to feed inland on the sugar beet harvest. And on the winter high tides, when the sea rolls in across the sprawling mudflats, tens of thousands of wading birds are pushed off their feeding banks and have to rise up onto the roost banks and islands.

The RSPB reserve at Snettisham, on Norfolk's west coast, is one of Britain's best birdwatching locations at any time of the year – but in winter the sheer numbers of birds make for a particularly spectacular sight. Huge numbers of waterfowl gather on the lagoons, while peregrines and hen harriers hunt on the salt marshes. There are four hides on the reserve – two accessible by wheelchair – and there is a programme of guided walks and a fascinating nature trail.

Snettisham makes a great base for exploring the quiet Norfolk countryside that spans out from the marshes. The village is surrounded by fenland, with a long stretch of undeveloped beach and a good smattering of pubs and small shops. The pace of life is slow and quiet, and fits perfectly with the vast skies and silent air that characterizes the RSPB reserve; broken only by the flocks of birds themselves.

There is more wildlife in the area than just birds, however. Snettisham Park (snettishampark.co.uk) is a working farm that offers a variety of experiences. Kids will love the chance to go on a deer safari – a 45-minute tractor ride through the deer park – and to get up close and personal with the sheep, goats, pigs and chickens that call the farm home. There are also children's art workshops and an adventure playground, ideal for 7–14 year olds.

Just up the road from Snettisham lies the Sandringham Estate (sandringham-estate.co.uk), the Queen's private country residence. Conservation is a central concern at Sandringham, and the stunning grounds – which are open to the public – have been lovingly maintained, with 5,000 trees and several miles of hedges planted each year. Alongside the gardens, the house is also open to visitors and there is a fascinating museum, with exhibits ranging from gifts given to the Queen on visits abroad to more quirky, personal mementos.

But it's the dramatic natural landscapes that are the real star in this corner of Norfolk. Take a walk along the Norfolk Coast Path to experience the vast empty seascapes, or follow the Nar Valley Way that begins from King's Lynn. Whenever you set out on foot you are bound to encounter wildlife at every turn – foxes, rabbits and other mammals, which make the most of the undisturbed countryside. This is a delightfully peaceful corner of the British Isles, perfect for a weekend escape from the pre-Christmas hubbub.

BELOW: Snow covers the banks at Snettisham. OPPOSITE INSET: The Eurasian Curlew is a common bird in Norfolk. BELOW: Flocks of knots take to the air as the tide comes in, providing one of Snettisham's great natural spectacles.

INFORMATION

STAY The **Twitchers' Retreat** (01485 543581; twitchers-retreat.co.uk) is a cosy B&B with (no surprise) a particular interest in birdwatching; notices about latest sightings and events are posted in the B&B daily. The **Lodge** (01485 532896; thelodgehunstanton.co.uk) in nearby Old Hunstanton is a sleek pub with an emphasis on locally sourced seafood and meats and comfortable rooms to retire to. For something more luxurious, the **Kings Head** (01485 578265; thekingshead hotel.co.uk) has 12 individually styled rooms and a renowned restaurant that opens out onto a picturesque terrace.

EAT The **Rose and Crown** (roseandcrownsnettisham.co.uk) is an award-winning classic country pub that specializes in local ales and hearty, traditional dishes. The **Orchard Tea Room** at Snettisham Park (snettishampark.co.uk) makes the most of its location, with home-made soups, cakes and sandwiches that utilize the farm's produce. For something a little more upscale, head to the **Eating Rooms** at Titchwell Manor (01485 210221; titchwellmanor.com), an informal dining room that opens out onto a terrace with beautiful sea views.

GETTING THERE Leave Kings Lynn on the A149 and look for the brown signs on the Snettisham bypass.

MORE INFO rspb.org.uk/reserves/guide/s/snettisham

OTHER GREAT BIRDWATCHING LOCATIONS
• Insh Marshes, Speyside (rspb.org)
• The Exe Estuary, Devon (exe-estuary.org)
• Slimbridge WWT Centre, Gloucestershire (wwt.org.uk)

51 Make a Pilgrimage
CANTERBURY, ENGLAND

Follow in the footsteps of centuries of pilgrims with a weekend in Kent's most picturesque city, dominated by the beautiful cathedral that is the home of the Church of England.

Winter in Canterbury is a magical time. The medieval cobbles are free of the tourist hordes that visit in the summer, and the air is thick with roasting chestnuts and the sound of buskers, who dot the busy, pedestrianized high street. On a crisp winter's afternoon the cathedral seems even more magnificent, and a stroll around the medieval precincts as dusk falls, with the sound of evensong echoing along the cloisters, is an unforgettable experience.

Present-day Canterbury is a mix of its various incarnations: place of pilgrimage, busy county town, heritage centre, student playground. The beauty of a weekend in Canterbury is it's easy to experience them all: a stroll around the ancient walls – believed to date back to Roman times – browsing the boutiques around the

OPPOSITE ABOVE LEFT: The delightfully crooked Sir John Boy's House. ABOVE RIGHT: Canterbury Cathedral seen from the University of Kent. BELOW: Magnificent Canterbury Cathedral.

Buttermarket, visiting the cathedral, dipping in and out of the numerous pubs and cafes that freckle the town.

For many visitors, Canterbury Cathedral (canterbury-cathedral.org) – home of the Church of England – is the biggest draw. Pilgrims have been making their way to this corner of Kent since the Middle Ages, and alongside the cathedral itself, the crypt and the tranquil precincts that link the church to the King's School can also be visited. Not always a place of peace, the cathedral is famous as the site of the murder of Thomas Becket in 1170, killed by four of Henry II's knights in the north-west transept.

Canterbury is equally famous for its role as the destination for Chaucer's pilgrims in *The Canterbury Tales*. Visitors to the town can learn more at the interactive exhibition of the same name (canterburytales.org.uk), which retells the stories and provides a useful insight into the city's past. For a broader insight, the Museum of Canterbury charts the city's development from Roman to Victorian times, and younger visitors will be delighted with the Rupert Bear exhibition.

But the real joy of a visit to this picturesque city is ambling around the streets and alleys and browsing in the small independent shops. The new Whitefriars development at the north end of the precinct has all the major chains, but the streets around Buttermarket are dotted with quirky, one-off shops. Indulge in handmade chocolates at Madame Oiseau (8 The Borough), browse the books in the 18th-century Chaucer Bookshop (6–7 Beer Cart Lane), or take the kids into the Winnie-the-Pooh Shop (19 Orange Street).

Outside the city, the Kent countryside lies lush with orchards and hop fields, dotted with country pubs that are perfect after a brisk winter walk. Visit medieval Chilham, with its picturesque high street or Chartham, tucked away in the valley of the river Stour. Pop into one of the local vineyards for a tasting or two, or head up to the coast at Whitstable or Herne Bay for a lazy seafood lunch by the sea. Whatever you're after for a winter weekend, Canterbury offers an unbeatable combination of 21st-century style and old-school tradition, all wrapped up in classic English landscapes.

INFORMATION

STAY The **Abode** (01227 766266; abodehotels.co.uk) is both the city's sleekest address and the best located – right on the high street. Chic bedrooms and a stylish eatery make this perfect for a romantic winter warmer. The nine rooms at luxury B&B the **House of Agnes** (01227 472185; houseofagnes.co.uk) are all individually styled, while the house itself dates back to the 13th century. If you fancy mixing in some countryside, **Beechborough B&B** (01227 832283; beechborough.com) offers comfortable rooms and indulgent breakfasts.

EAT A Canterbury institution, **Marlowes** (01227 461294; marlowesrestaurant.co.uk) has been serving up wicked margaritas, sizzling fajitas and gargantuan desserts for over 30 years. Indulge in traditional British treats such as a 'huffkin' – a huge soft roll crammed full of local ham or bacon and eggs – at **Tiny Tim's Tea Room** (01227 450793; tinytimstearoom.co.uk). Whether you're after food for a picnic, or a sit-down lunch, the **Goods Shed** (01227 459153; thegoodsshed.net) is a must-visit; the only daily farmers' market in the UK, situated in a disused goods shed, crammed full of local produce.

GETTING THERE Take the A28 from the A2 and follow signs to Canterbury.

MORE INFO canterbury.co.uk

OTHER PLACES OF PILGRIMAGE
• Glastonbury Tor, Somerset (glastonbury.co.uk)
• Ynys Mon, the Isle of Anglesey (visitanglesey.co.uk)
• Island of Iona, Scotland (isle-of-iona.com)

52 See the Northern Lights
NAIRN, SCOTLAND

Head to the northerly coast of the Scottish mainland for a chance to see one of nature's most awe-inspiring spectacles, the aurora borealis.

There are few more spectacular sights on the planet than an inky night sky glowing scarlet, green and gold as the Northern Lights shimmer and gleam in the winter air.

BELOW: *In Scotland the Northern Lights are often known as the 'merrie dancers' and considered to be a sign of unsettled weather.*

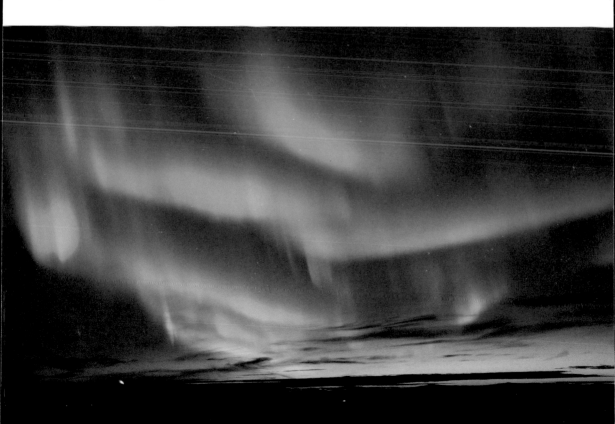

A natural phenomenon that occurs only in extreme northern and southern latitudes, the polar lights are caused by the solar winds colliding with gas particles in the Earth's magnetic fields. The result is a spectacular display of undulating waves of colour that ripple gold and jade-green across the sky.

The Moray Firth on the north-east coast is one of the best places in the UK to see the Northern Lights, and the former fishing port of Nairn makes a great base for exploring the Scottish Highlands. For the best and clearest view of the aurora, drive into the countryside beyond the town or walk out along the beach – the less light pollution, the clearer the aurora will be.

Nairn was once such a large town that it was said different languages were spoken at

ABOVE: Cawdor Castle has evolved over 600 years and in a number of architectural styles.

either end of it: Gaelic-speaking crofters at the landward end and Scots-speaking fishermen by the sea. Modern Nairn still has two halves – land and seaside – split by the main Inverness-Elgin road.

With the nights given over to watching the Northern Lights (although it is important to point out that there is never any guarantee of seeing them), there is plenty to do in the area during the day. Famous for its long, sandy beaches, in Victorian times the town was known as the Brighton of the North. Although the winter months may be a little chilly for swimming there are some stunning walks along the beachfront. One

INFORMATION

route from the harbour leads inland to the spectacular castle at Cawdor, from where there are five natural trails to ramble along. A shorter circular route leads from the beach into Delnies Wood before looping back to the shore.

A walk in an easterly direction along Nairn's sandy beach leads to the RSPB reserve at Culbin Sands, home to up to 12,000 wintering birds, including lapwings, redshanks, oystercatchers and teals. The reserve has a wonderfully remote feel and offers the chance to see some more unusual species, including ringed plovers and velvet scoters.

There are some spectacular historic sites to visit in the area: Cawdor (cawdorcastle.com) is a 14th-century castle surrounded by beautifully landscaped gardens, Brodie Castle (nts.org.uk) is a stunning 16th-century tower house filled with art and antiques, while the ruins of Urquhart Castle (historic-scotland.gov.uk) remain an impressive site, in a spectacular location on the banks of Loch Ness.

The area around Nairn is also famous for its golf courses: the town has two championship courses – the Nairn Golf Club, which dates back to 1887, and the slightly younger Nairn Dunbar Golf Club, which has been described by renowned golf commentator Peter Alliss as one of Scotland's 'hidden golfing gems'. Some 13km (8 miles) from the town, the Castle Stuart Golf Links is a new course which has already hosted the Barclays Scottish Open.

PICTURE CREDITS

Abergavenny Food Festival (abergavennyfoodfestival .com): p.107tr; Ace Adventure (aceadventures.co.uk): p.155tl; Alamy: p.12–13 (Carole Drake), 35 (Wig Worland), 36 (Liquid Light), 37 (Jane Roberts), 40tr (Ian Goodrich), 46 (John Farnham), 48 (JTB Communications, Inc.), 71tr (Geoffrey Morgan),109 (Guy Edwardes Photography), 118 (Lee Karen Stow), 127tr (Tracey Coupland), 127b (Matt Cardy), 129 (Alex Fieldhouse), 141 (John Morris), 143b (FLPA), 174 (N8urPs),184 (Oliver Smart), 185tr (Oliver Smart), 185b (Chris Gomersall), 186tr (Peter de Clerq); Alnwick Castle and The Alnwick Garden (alnwickgarden.com): p.157, 158; Bamburgh Castle (bamburghcastle.com): p.159 (Nick McCann); Bath Tourism (visitbath.co.uk): p.111tl; Bettys Café Tearooms (www.bettys.co.uk): p.19 tl & tr; Broads Authority (broads-authority.gov.uk): p.135, 136; Bristol City Council (bristol.gov.uk): p.92 (Christian Lathom Sharp); Bristol International Balloon Fiesta (bristolballoonfiesta.co.uk): p.1; Brogdale Collections (brogdalecollections.co.uk): p.39; Cairngorm Mountain (cairngormmountain.co.uk): p.155 tr & b; Cawdor Castle (cawdorcastle.com): p.190; Chester Grosvenor Hotel (chestergrosvenor.com): p.99; City of Lincoln Council (lincoln.gov.uk): p.161; Covent Garden London (coventgardenlondonuk.com): p.2–3, 153; Cowmans Famous Sausage Shop, Clitheroe, Lancs.: p.145; Cowes Week Ltd (CWL): p.101 (Rick Tomlinson), 103 (Rick Tomlinson); Dedham Vale AONB and Stour Valley Project (dedhamvalestourvalley.org): p.43tr; Deli on the Square, Ludlow (delionthesquare.co.uk): p.25tr; Derby City Council (derby.gov.uk): p.163bl; Derby QUAD (derbyquad.co.uk): p.164 (Graham Lucas Commons); Derwent Mills Partnership: p.163 (by permission of The Derwent Mills Partnership); Destination Bristol (visitbristol.co.uk): p.90–91 (Carl Whitham), 93; Drayton Manor Theme Park (draytonmanor.co.uk): p.29; Edward Rokita: p. 71tr ; Everards Brewery Ltd. (everards.co.uk): p.165; Forest Holidays (forestholidays.co.uk): p.51, 53; Getty Images: p.31, 181; Gjt6: p.144; Graham Well: p.143tr; Harrogate Culture and Tourism (harrogate.gov.uk): p.19b (by kind permission of Mike Hine); Ironbridge Gorge Museum (ironbridge.org.uk): p.95tr; Isle of Wight Council and islandbreaks.co.uk): p.23; Istockphoto: p.14 (Joanna Glab), 69 (Scott Hortop), 81 (Barry Thomas), 82tl (Lisbeth Landström), 85b (Paul Fawcett), 88 (Tom Viggars), 95tl (Steve Geer), 117 (Radomir Rezny), 121 (Ai-Lan Lee), 125 (Paul Tilley), 139tl, (ChrisAt), 146 (Steve Wignall), 168 (David Hills), 171b (Peter Elvidge); Kielder Observatory (kielderobservatory.org): p.133tr; Kielder Water and Forest Park Development Trust (visitkielder.com): p.133b; Landmark Trust (landmarktrust.org.uk): p. 32tr (Stuart Leavy), 33 (Stuart Leavy); Liamcrouse1: p.120; Ludlow Castle (ludlowcastle.com): p.25tr; Ludlow Town Council (ludlow.gov.uk): p.25tl; Mercury PR: p.65; Michael Maggs: p.32b; Minack Theatre (www.minack.com): p. 87; Monkey Forest at Trentham (trentham-monkey-forest.com): p.27; morebyless: p.124; Mount Ephraim Gardens (mountephraimgardens.co.uk): p.40b; National Marine Aquarium (national-aquarium.co.uk): p.78bl; New Inn, Shalfleet (thenew-inn.co.uk): p.22; NorfolkBroads.com: p.137 © NorfolkBroads.com; Photolibrary: p.16, 43b, 45, 52, 74, 139b; PPL Ltd.: p.6, 7, 8, 9, 58, 60 tr & b, 61, 62, 112–13, 115, 176, 178 (x3), 179; Plymouth City Council (plymouth.gov.uk): p.77, 79; Rex Features: p.182 (Nick Randall); Smith609; Smith609: p.82br; stock. xchng: p.21 (Ines Mad), 56 (Jet Steverink), 102, (Alan Earley), 130 (David Anderson), 186b (Marek Bernat); Scilly Tourism (simplyscilly.co.uk): p.66; Scottish Natural Heritage (snh.gov.uk): p.83 (Glen Tyler); Shutterstock: p.2–3 (fcarucci), 17 (Gail Johnson), 50 (David Hughes), 54–55 (James Cameron), 67 (Lichtmeister), 73 (David Hughes), 75 (David Hughes), 95b (Groome), 104–05 (Martin Fowler), 119 (Jeff Banke), 123 (Peter R. Foster, IDMA), 147 (Jane McIlroy), 167 (godrick), 171tr (Samuel Roberts), 173 (ronfromyork), 186tl (Guy Erwood), 189; Stopham Vineyard, West Sussex (stophamvineyard.co.uk) p.68; Trentham Estate (trentham.co.uk): p.28; Toby Thurston: p.57; Visit Chester and Cheshire (visitchester.com): p.97, 98; Visit Cornwall (visitcornwall.com): p.89 (Paul Watts); Visit London (visitlondon.com): p.148–49, 150–51; Visit Wales: p.107b © Crown copyright (2011); Visit Wiltshire (visitwiltshire .co.uk) p.111tr (Bryn Jones); Warwick Lister-Kaye: p.166; Wasdale Head Inn (wasdale.com): p.85tr; Welcome to Yorkshire (yorkshire.com): p.174; West Dorset District Council (dorsetforyou.com): p.171tl; West Somerset Council (westsomersetonline.gov.uk): p.131; Westons Cider (westons-cider.co.uk): p.139tr, 140; Gynn Williams (sinfin .net): p.71b; Zoological Society of London (zsl.org): p.46br.